SCHOLASTIC

P9-DWW-470

Using Read-Alouds to Teach
VOCABULARY

Research-Based Strategies and Model Lessons for Using
Fiction and Nonfiction Books to Build Children's Vocabulary
and Improve Their Reading, Writing, and Speaking Skills

Karen J. Kindle

New York • Toronto • London • Auckland • Sydney
Mexico City • New Delhi • Hong Kong • Buenos Aires

Teaching *Resources*

CALGARY PUBLIC LIBRARY

MAY   2011

Dedication

To Jason, Erika, and David

Scholastic grants teachers permission to photocopy the reproducible pages from this book for classroom use.
No other part of this publication may be reproduced in whole or in part, or stored in a retrieval system, or transmitted in any
form or by any means, electronic, mechanical, photocopying, recording, or otherwise, without permission of the publisher.
For information regarding permission, write to Scholastic Inc., 557 Broadway, New York, NY 10012.

Editor: Sarah Glasscock
Acquisition Editor: Joanna Davis-Swing
Interior Designer: Sarah Morrow

Copyright © 2011 by Karen J. Kindle
All rights reserved. Published by Scholastic Inc.
Printed in the U.S.A.
ISBN: 978-0-545-16513-6

1 2 3 4 5 6 7 8 9 10   40   18 17 16 15 14 13 12 11

Contents

CHAPTER 4 Constructing Vocabulary Units Based on Read-Alouds 34

CHAPTER 5 Nonfiction Read-Aloud Units 44

CHAPTER 6 Fiction Read-Aloud Units 89

References 125

Children's Literature Cited 128

Introduction

In a recently published study of curricula used by schools receiving Early Reading First funds, Neuman and Dwyer (2009) concluded that "little exists right now that is helpful to teachers who want to do a better job of providing explicit instruction in vocabulary to young children" (p. 391). Teachers using these curricula would need to provide supplemental instruction for students to make the required gains in vocabulary development.

With the strong research links seen between vocabulary and reading achievement, the lack of focused attention to vocabulary in published materials is troubling. You would be hard pressed to find a teacher or administrator who would not express the belief that vocabulary was important, yet observations of their practices might show a different picture. Neuman and Dwyer (2009) state it well. "There was a general pattern of 'acknowledging' the importance of vocabulary but sporadic attention to actually addressing this skill intentionally" (p. 392).

Why is this happening? Perhaps it is due to the increased focus on academic achievement in primary classrooms. Formal instruction in literacy skills is now common in kindergarten (Hiebert, 1988). Students are routinely tested for alphabet recognition, phonological awareness, sight word knowledge, and early decoding skills. There are many opinions about this practice, but an unfortunate side effect of structured skills instruction is a tendency to view early literacy development as the mastery of a set of discrete items or skills. In efforts to ensure that students are competent decoders, other critically important but untested components of literacy such as oral language and vocabulary can be neglected (Juel, Biancarosa, Coker, & Deffes, 2003). A balance must be struck, for although word identification and vocabulary knowledge are both necessary for reading comprehension (Mason, Stahl, Au, & Herman, 2003, p. 914), neither component is sufficient in itself.

The process of researching, selecting, and securing funding for supplemental programs is lengthy and arduous in most districts. For students who are learning English as a second language and for children of poverty, the need is urgent. Outside the school setting, these students are less likely to be exposed to the type of vocabulary and language needed for academic success. As recommendations for materials and programs are made and the pros and cons of prospective programs are debated, it is up to the individual teacher to do what she or he can to ensure that students get the critical vocabulary instruction they need to be successful in school.

The approach to vocabulary instruction described in this volume represents one such attempt, born of the conviction that something needed to be done, and the unwillingness to wait until a curriculum was imposed from above. It represents a common-sense approach to incorporating vocabulary instruction into every aspect of the day, called *vocabulary infusion*. This particular volume focuses on the use of read-alouds as the source and inspiration for vocabulary instruction.

CHAPTER 1

Why Use Read-Alouds for Teaching Vocabulary?

"I like to read to my class, but there is so much to do, I just don't have time to read aloud very often." This is a common sentiment voiced in today's primary classrooms. Teachers are overwhelmed and sometimes frustrated by the many lessons they need to teach each day. These feelings are compounded by assessment schedules that require them to work with students to individually assess a wide variety of skills, which leaves even less time for instruction. It is easy to see why reading aloud gets relegated to a transition activity to fill a few moments after lunch or before students leave for the day. In most classrooms, more language arts time is spent in skills activities such as letter naming than in listening to the teacher read (Hiebert, 1988).

There are also misconceptions about read-alouds among administrators. I had a principal who actually told teachers he did not want to see instructional time wasted by reading aloud. In his mind, read-alouds were of little or no value in developing literacy skills and so shouldn't be taking up valuable instructional time. To be fair, there are a lot of teachers who put little thought into their read-alouds, simply grabbing a book off the shelf to read with no advance planning. This is *not* the type of read-aloud that will impact vocabulary development or reading comprehension.

The Achievement Gap

Politicians and educators are united in their desire to close the gap in academic performance between white and minority students. The reading assessment scores from the 2007 National Assessment of Educational Progress (NAEP) showed some narrowing of the gap nationwide, but clearly we have a long way to go. On the fourth-grade reading assessment, no changes in the gap were noted in 10 states (Vanneman, Hamilton, Anderson, & Rahman, 2009). As we continue our efforts to improve reading instruction for all students, but particularly for those at risk of failure, the potential of read-alouds should be explored.

The positive benefits of read-alouds are well established in the research literature. In a shared reading context, students learn about print concepts (Tompkins, 2006) that will support their early reading efforts. Reading aloud builds vocabulary and background knowledge and exposes students to language that may differ significantly from their everyday speech. In fact, children's books have more rare words per hundred than is typically heard in conversations between college-educated adults (Hayes & Ahrens, 1988). Students develop comprehension skills as the conversation and interactions that occur during a read-aloud teach them how to construct meaning from text (Morrow, Freitag, & Gambrell, 2009).

Read-alouds are developmentally appropriate and part of the instructional routines recommended by the joint position statement developed by two leading organizations, the National Association for the Education of Young Children (NAEYC) and the International Reading Association (IRA) published in 1998. Students who are read to understand stories better, notice more picture clues, make more sophisticated inferences, and tell more connected stories (Hiebert, 1988). Students who are read to typically have more interest in looking at books independently, imitating the reading behaviors they have seen modeled.

Read-alouds also serve an important role in the literacy development of culturally and linguistically diverse children. As teachers read engaging texts, they serve as "literate role models," sharing their own love of books and reading with their students (Au, 1998, p. 21). For some of these students, such role models may not be available to them outside of the school setting (Au, 1998).

The Role of Read-Alouds in a Balanced Literacy Program

Read-alouds are included as a vital component in most models of balanced literacy instruction. They are a powerful tool for modeling the use of comprehension strategies as the teacher demonstrates his or her own thinking while reading. They expose students to a wide range of text genres and authors that they might otherwise not encounter (Fountas & Pinnell, 2001).

I am concerned about the perception that reading aloud is the "soft" part of the balanced literacy model that includes read-aloud, shared reading, guided reading, and independent reading, and thus is somehow optional. Most proponents of balanced literacy suggest that even though the focus of instruction may shift from one area to another as students develop their reading skills, all four components are important to include as they all serve different purposes and are not intended to be sequential.

Shared reading is critical for teaching students print concepts. It is typically done with enlarged print such as a big book or a chart. As the teacher reads, he or she might point to each word to model one-to-one matching or directionality and return sweep. Important concepts such as locating the front and back of the book and turning pages are demonstrated. Students may be asked to locate specific items that have been taught such as a capital letter or key sight words. The texts for shared reading are usually simple and predictable and are often familiar in order to help students make the voice-print match.

Guided reading serves a far different function. Fountas and Pinnell (1996) state that in guided reading "teachers can show children how to read and can support children as they read" (p. 1). The teacher provides the appropriate scaffolds so that each child is able to develop and use effective strategies for reading a text that is challenging yet manageable, within the supportive context of the guided reading lesson.

Independent reading gives students the opportunity to practice reading. Students develop fluency by reading and rereading texts that present little to no challenge for them. Students get to revisit old favorites, and to pursue their individual interests.

Read-alouds serve several important roles in a balanced literacy classroom. From the perspective of this book, they provide an essential vehicle for vocabulary development as students are exposed to novel words in the supportive and engaging medium of picture books and other texts. Second, they are perfect for modeling comprehension strategies. As you read the book to your students, you can use think-aloud modeling techniques to demonstrate how you construct meaning as you read. Third, read-alouds expose students to texts that are beyond their independent reading level, which builds background knowledge, acquaints them with various language structures, and provides a scaffold to later independent readings of the same text. Read-alouds are somewhat unique because they are the only place where students get to hear wonderful stories that are beyond their ability to read on their own. They are exposed to rich vocabulary, complex sentence structures, and figurative language. Because the "work" of decoding is done by the teacher, the child is able to use all his or her cognitive energy for understanding the text. Students who are beginning readers will not be exposed to the rich vocabulary of stories when they are limited to those texts they can read independently (Au, 1998).

Finally, read-alouds provide a model for students of fluent, expressive reading and are useful in building motivation. When you read a book to the class with excitement and expression, it often becomes highly sought-after during independent reading times. I can still remember making my mother take me to the library to get *Johnny Tremain* after my fifth-grade teacher read it to the class. Through her expressive reading, I was drawn to a text that I might never have chosen for myself. A friend of mine who is a school librarian told me that she can usually tell which books a teacher has been reading aloud to her or his class by the number of student requests for particular books and authors.

Using Read-Alouds to Teach Vocabulary © 2011 by Karen J. Kindle, Scholastic Teaching Resources

Vocabulary Development and Reading Achievement

The research community is in agreement that there is a strong relationship between vocabulary and reading comprehension (Baumann, Kame'enui, & Ash, 2003), and the National Reading Panel identified vocabulary as one of the five core components of reading (2000). It seems so obvious: In order to comprehend what you are reading, you need to understand what the words mean. Being able to decode or pronounce them accurately is necessary but not sufficient for comprehension. Vocabulary represents more than just words—it represents knowledge (Neuman & Dwyer, 2009). Students who know a lot of words also know more about their world.

We also know that vocabulary size is predictive of later reading achievement (Biemiller, 2001) and that children who grow up in poverty enter school having heard far fewer words than their more advantaged classmates (Hart & Risely, 1995). Students who do not have sufficient vocabulary face increased difficulties with standardized tests (Chall & Snow, 1988), making vocabulary deficits an important factor in the achievement gap (Hirsch, 2005). On standardized assessment, children from low socioeconomic backgrounds are "over-represented in the group of students with weak vocabulary knowledge" (Juel et al., 2003, p. 14).

The exact relationship between vocabulary and reading achievement is a bit less clear in the literature, but limited vocabulary knowledge might be thought of as "both a cause and an effect of poor achievement in reading" (Chiappone, 2006, p. 306). Students who have strong vocabulary knowledge tend to have an easier time learning to read. Students who become proficient and motivated readers build their vocabulary as they encounter new words in text. Proficient readers read more, gaining more practice and learning increasing numbers of words, which in turn improves their comprehension. This upward spiral of achievement is the result of the Matthew Effect (Stanovich, 1986), a phenomenon named for the biblical passage containing the proverb, "The rich get richer and the poor get poorer." Unfortunately, the converse is also true: Students who struggle with reading read less. When they do read, they choose simpler texts that provide less exposure to novel vocabulary. Because these children read less, they have fewer opportunities to improve their reading, thus initiating the downward spiral of the Matthew Effect. Additionally, in a further application of the Matthew Effect, Neuman and Dwyer (2009) also suggest that the more words a child knows, the easier it is to learn more words.

For young students, read-alouds present a natural, developmentally appropriate way for them to expand their vocabulary. The majority of words that they acquire are not learned through direct instruction, but rather through their language environments and independent reading. In read-alouds, students hear novel words in supportive contexts, often with illustrations that help convey word meaning. Read-alouds have the potential to make a positive impact on the vocabulary learning trajectory by increasing students' exposure to rich and complex words.

Vocabulary and English Language Learners

Our classrooms are increasing in their diversity at a record pace. Almost every teacher will have some students who are limited in their English proficiency, and in some classrooms the number of different home languages represented is amazing. Nationally, 37 percent of K–12 students were characterized as culturally, linguistically, or ethnically different by the National Center for Education Statistics (2000) and that number is growing. Within this group, there is also significant diversity. Avalos (2006) rightly points out that ELLs not only come from different language groups but also "have varying needs *within* their language groups" (p. 62).

Parents of ELL students are often counseled by well-intentioned teachers to speak only English at home to accelerate language acquisition. Unfortunately, this strategy can create students who are not only limited in their English proficiency but also in their home language as well. With the strong links between thought and language (Vygotsky, 1962), children with limited oral language skills in their home language find learning literacy skills in school to be a challenge. The relationship between oral language proficiency and reading achievement (Nation & Snowling, 2004) highlights the critical importance of well-developed language skills regardless of which language is dominant.

One of the principles of ELL instruction is comprehensible input (Krashen, 1985). Comprehensible input involves a conscious selection of words and language structures that make meaning accessible to students. To make language instruction comprehensible, teachers use a variety of strategies such as modeling, visual aids, and explicit instruction (Avalos, 2006). Read-alouds, particularly when strategies for developing vocabulary are built in, help with vocabulary acquisition because they increase comprehensibility. It is also critical to make language experiences meaningful by giving students opportunities to use new vocabulary and language patterns in authentic contexts (Avalos, 2006). The strategies described in this book do exactly that as students are exposed to target terms, first within the supportive context of the read-aloud and then through multiple exposures in authentic ways.

Chiappone (2006) suggests that there are seven principles that should guide vocabulary instruction for all students, including ELLs. All of these principles can be incorporated in an instructional plan that introduces vocabulary within a read-aloud and then infuses target vocabulary into conversations and instruction throughout the day.

Principle 1: Develop awareness of stages of word knowledge.

Principle 2: Build experiential background for students.

Principle 3: Make word learning related to students' backgrounds.

Using Read-Alouds to Teach Vocabulary © 2011 by Karen J. Kindle, Scholastic Teaching Resources

Principle 4: Develop depth of meaning through multiple sources and
               repeated exposures.

Principle 5: Foster appreciation and enthusiasm for word learning.

Principle 6: Teach strategies to build independent word learning.

Principle 7: Teach words in context. (p. 302)

Read-alouds also provide opportunities for ELLs to acquire both Basic Interpersonal Communication Skills (BICS) and Cognitive Academic Language Proficiency (CALP), two constructs of great importance in the language-acquisition literature. BICS includes daily conversational language. In read-alouds, students hear repetitive phrases or models of conversational speech. For example, in *Brown Bear, Brown Bear, What Do You See?* (Martin, 1983), they hear the phrases *what do you see* and *I see a* ____ . Both sentences provide a useful language pattern in conversational English. Students can begin learning academic language early through supportive read-alouds in the content areas. Through read-alouds of *It's Pumpkin Time!* (Hall, 1994), they can learn academic language such as *seeds, roots, vine,* and *flower.*

Vocabulary infusion is my approach to building vocabulary throughout the day by creating a learning environment that values words and capitalizing on each teachable moment. The next chapter describes this concept in detail so that you can begin the process of effective vocabulary instruction for all your young learners.

CHAPTER 2

The Infusion Concept

During the course of my education, I have taken classes in German, French, and Spanish. I studied hard and always made good grades on exams, which were filled with lists of vocabulary words. Today, I remember only a little Spanish and almost nothing of French and German. Most of us know from experience that memorizing a list of words and definitions for a Friday test has little long-term value. Unless we learn words in meaningful contexts and have many opportunities to use them in authentic ways, long-term word knowledge is unlikely.

The infusion approach to vocabulary development seeks to maximize word learning by providing context and opportunity. As important as read-alouds are, some research suggests that they are not enough to result in significant vocabulary growth. There is, however, also significant research indicating that more purposeful approaches do in fact have positive results (Juel et al., 2003). The additional exposures and efforts to teach word meaning in infusion help address this issue by providing those additional opportunities to engage with word meaning. A more focused approach to vocabulary is especially important for ELLs, who may need more direct instruction to learn words than their classmates (Mason et al., 2003).

What Is Vocabulary Infusion?

Infusion is based on the idea that children's vocabulary is built through multiple exposures to words in multiple contexts. Although it is not a program, it is a purposeful approach in which the teacher seeks to incorporate "incidental" exposure to target words throughout the day. The teacher infuses target vocabulary at every opportunity, providing students with multiple opportunities to hear and use new words in supportive and meaningful contexts. The teacher's enthusiasm for interesting words becomes contagious, fostering the development of *word consciousness* (Graves, 2006). Students who have this heightened awareness of words become curious about or attuned to unfamiliar and unusual words (Carlisle, 2000), triggering the word learning process. "Vocabulary knowledge takes place through word play and talk about language as well as through wide-ranging opportunities to express, hear, and read new words in meaningful contexts" (Mason et al., 2003, p. 914).

Although this text focuses on infusing words that have been introduced in the context of read-alouds, infusion is not limited to a discrete list of words, but should be part of an overall mind-set of the teacher's approach to instruction and interaction throughout the day. A more in-depth explanation of how to infuse vocabulary into daily routines can be found in *Teaching Vocabulary in the K–2 Classroom: Easy Strategies for Infusing Vocabulary Learning into Morning Meetings, Transitions, Centers, and More* (Kindle, 2008).

Learning More About Words ::

Infusion is about learning more words, but also learning more about words. Word knowledge is acquired gradually through repeated exposures. Each time we encounter a novel word, either in print or in our language environment, we gather a little more information about the word's meaning and how it is used. Most models of word learning (i.e. Dale, 1965; Graves, 1986; Nagy & Scott, 2000) include some version of the following stages:

1. **Recognition:** The first step in learning a new word is to identify it as an unfamiliar word. This triggers cognitive activity as the child attempts to construct meaning by assigning a tentative meaning to the word. Carey (1978) calls this initial effort *fast mapping*.

2. **Use in limited contexts:** The child begins to use the word in limited contexts. For example, he or she may respond to a question about a story and use the new word in the answer. The child may recognize the word *iguana* as a character from the story *Mañana, Iguana* (Paul, 2004), but not realize that an *iguana* is a real animal.

3. **Knowledge of alternate meanings and uses:** In this stage, the child learns to use the word in a variety of contexts, as well as alternate meanings for the word. The child learns that the word *scoop* can refer to ice cream on a cone, the utensil used to get that ice cream out of the carton, or the action involved in the process.

4. **Understanding how the word fits into the larger lexicon:** The final stage of word knowledge is reached when the child understands the word in depth, including connotations and pragmatics, the way language is used in different settings and for different purposes.

Immersion Versus Infusion ::

It is obvious from the amazing rate at which children acquire new words—an average of eight to ten new words each day—that most new words are acquired through incidental exposure rather than through direct instruction. Students who regularly hear language that is rich with interesting and novel words tend to have vocabularies characterized by depth and breadth. And so it makes sense that if we expose students with meager vocabulary to rich language environments, they will learn new words. This premise is the basis for the principle of *immersion*, a term often used in vocabulary and language development (Genesee, 1985), particularly in the context of second-language acquisition. The concept of immersion suggests that if we surround or bathe children in language, they will pick it up. Immersion does result in increases in vocabulary and language (Cummins, 1983), but not necessarily at the rates needed to narrow the vocabulary gap, which research indicates increase over time (Biemiller, 2001).

How is infusion different from immersion? Infusion combines the principles of immersion, comprehensible input, and vocabulary development. The teacher creates the rich language environment, incorporates strategies that make rich language comprehensible to the students on a continual basis, and provides multiple opportunities for students to use new words in authentic written and oral communication.

Recently, I was watching a cooking show and the host was creating a red pepper-infused olive oil. She didn't just immerse the peppers in the oil—she cut them up, put them in the oil, and then heated the oil to get every possible bit of flavor infused into the oil. The process was simple, but the few extra steps and intentionality on the part of the cook made all the difference in the results.

I believe that vocabulary infusion works the same way. Rather than just surrounding students with words and hoping they will soak them up, the infusion teacher approaches the task with intention and focus. Words are targeted for instruction, and the teacher takes deliberate actions to be sure that students see and hear these words in a variety of contexts. Vocabulary learning becomes a goal and not a by-product.

Intentionality and Intensity ::

Intentionality and intensity are the defining characteristics of infusion. Intentionality is manifested in the purposeful manner in which the teacher selects words for focus and incorporates them into as many contexts as possible to provide students with the multiple exposures and opportunities to use the words in authentic conversation and literacy activities. Although powerful teachable moments do occur spontaneously in classrooms, their frequency will be increased with a teacher who approaches vocabulary development with a sense of purpose and balances spontaneity with thoughtful instructional moments.

Intentionality is evident when the teacher seeks and finds opportunities to infuse target terms into classroom discourse throughout the day. The additional exposures provide opportunities for students to confirm, revise, and/or refine their word knowledge as words are presented in multiple and flexible contexts. For example, when reading *Snowmen at Night* (Buehner, 2002), you might provide a quick synonym for *tuckered out*: "that means they are tired." Later in the day after the students have had recess or PE time, you might comment that they look all *tuckered out*, just like the snowmen. If you read *The Wind*

Blew (Hutchins, 1993) on a windy day, show them how the wind is *whipping* the leaves off the trees, or how it *swept* up the dirt under the swings.

Intensity is manifested in several ways as well. First, as the teacher clearly demonstrates his or her own interest in and love of words, intense interest in novel words is likely to be seen in students as well. They notice and attend to what we show we value. Secondly, intensity is achieved through frequency as students are exposed to novel terms many times and in varied contexts. Students learn about the words during the read-aloud, but then see and hear those same words again in a math word problem. The teacher uses them yet again during a science or social studies lesson. This intensity of instruction helps solidify word knowledge.

Research Support

Research indicates that children acquire vocabulary at an astonishing rate and that most of these words are learned incidentally. Unfortunately, the words they learn are not always the language that will support literacy development in school. Almost every parent has asked his or her child at some time, "Where did you hear that?" when the child uses a questionable word or phrase! In most cases, words are learned gradually as children hear novel words used repeatedly in meaningful contexts (Nagy & Scott, 2000). Repetition and meaning contexts are an integral part of the infusion concept.

Mason et al. (2003) identified three principles of vocabulary development in their extensive review of the literature. The infusion approach in conjunction with read-alouds is consistent with all three. First, instruction should include both definitional and contextual information. As a story is read aloud, new terms are presented in context and that context is supportive in its familiarity. Teachers provide definitional information through their actions and elaborations. Second, students must be actively engaged in constructing word meanings. Infusion activities help students see the relationships between new and known words, understand similarities and differences, and identify other contexts in which the word might be used. Finally, discussion should be used to teach word meanings. In the discussion related to read-alouds and in the subsequent infusion activities, students are engaged in talking about word meanings, sharing their thinking, and explaining their reasoning.

How Do I Start With Infusion?

Creating a rich language environment in your classroom is not difficult, but it is not automatic. Infusion initially requires conscious effort and attention, but you will quickly find that it becomes a habitual way of teaching and talking to your students. Once you begin looking for ways to infuse vocabulary into your daily routines, you will be amazed at the endless opportunities.

Students naturally imitate the vocabulary and language patterns they hear regularly in their language environment. The idea of infusion is to capitalize on the language acquisition processes already in place by consciously and deliberately adding rich, mature vocabulary. As an ESL teacher, I had the good fortune to spend a significant amount of time in a kindergarten class that was taught by a British woman who had just arrived in the country. I was a bit surprised one afternoon to hear a little Pakistani girl ask her teacher, "Shall I put my rubbish in the bin?" I am quite confident that the teacher did not directly teach the words *rubbish* and *bin*, but her consistent use of that language pattern provided a strong model that was absorbed by the child.

You may find it extremely enlightening to tape-record your teaching and classroom interactions for a day and listen with vocabulary in mind. Is your discourse rich with interesting and unusual words? Or do you tend to keep your language simple and businesslike? Notice how students' speech patterns tend to mimic your own. Identify places where you could have infused some vocabulary to enrich the language environment for your students.

This book specifically explores how vocabulary from read-alouds can be infused into other parts of the day, so that words learned within the context of the read-aloud can be reinforced in multiple ways. In Chapter 3, specific strategies for developing vocabulary before, during, and after your read-alouds are presented. Chapter 4 provides a framework for designing vocabulary units based on read-alouds. The last two chapters contain sample units for a variety of nonfiction and fiction texts.

Using Read-Alouds to Teach Vocabulary © 2011 by Karen J. Kindle, Scholastic Teaching Resources

Effective Strategies for Vocabulary Development

The strategies presented in this chapter are consistent with recommendations for vocabulary instruction for all students, including ELLs and students with less developed vocabulary. Although many students seem to acquire extensive vocabularies through incidental exposure to rich language environments, other students need support to learn unfamiliar words. For these students, just reading aloud may not be enough. Visual cues provided by labeling, multiple readings of the story, multiple exposures to the words in a variety of contexts, and visual imagery such as gestures and facial expressions are effective in helping students learn new words during reading (Morrow et al., 2009).

Students who are in the process of learning English do not always participate in discussions related to books that have been read aloud. Read-alouds *can* provide a powerful vehicle for language acquisition for these students *if* they are guided to connect with the text in meaningful ways and to see the connections or relationships between words and ideas (Hickman & Pollard-Durodola, 2009).

The ELLs in any given class will vary in terms of their language proficiency. Some students might be at a preproduction or silent stage in which they are listening and observing but make few if any attempts at expression. During this stage, students benefit from hearing the language of the read-aloud, and certain strategies such as labeling and gestures provide links between words and their meanings. As students progress in their language acquisition, they benefit from repeated read-alouds, as each reading gives them additional opportunities to revise and refine their interpretations of meaning. Read-alouds also provide these learners with mature language models that are presented in a supportive context.

Teachers can support vocabulary and language development by several means: visual support, such as pictures or graphic organizers, movement and gestures, and linguistic emphasis in which pitch and stress are used to highlight key words or phrases (Hickman & Pollard-Durodola, 2009). These strategies can be effectively incorporated before or after reading as well as embedded during the reading of the text.

Before Reading

Before beginning a read-aloud, teachers can help activate prior knowledge by leading discussions about what students already know about the topic (Hickman & Pollard-Durodola, 2009). For example, before reading *Dig Dig Digging* (Mayo & Ayliffe, 2001), a teacher might ask students about different kinds of construction vehicles they have seen working in their neighborhoods and what they think each one does. Graphic organizers, such as K-W-L charts, can be used to record the discussions and to document learning.

Prior knowledge can also be activated through picture walks, in which the teacher guides students in examining the illustrations. Assessing the children's prior knowledge helps the teacher identify which words and concepts are familiar, and which will require further instruction. As the students preview the illustrations, questions can be asked to assess vocabulary knowledge. For example, during a picture walk of *In the Small, Small Pond* (Fleming, 1993), the teacher might ask questions such as the following:

- *Look at this large, white bird. Does anyone know what it is called?*

- *Have you seen birds like this near ponds or lakes?*

Key ideas that are essential for story comprehension might be pretaught so students are able to construct meaning during the reading. While not specifically related to vocabulary, these concepts are vital to constructing meaning during the reading. For example, ELLs who have not experienced Halloween would benefit from a discussion that explains this celebration in order to understand texts such as *It's Pumpkin Time!* (Hall, 1994). You can also develop concepts by brainstorming examples. For instance, as students hear examples of animals that are mammals, they refine their understanding of the defining characteristics of mammals.

During Reading

Although research suggests that children can learn new words just from hearing them in the read-aloud (Biemiller & Boote, 2006), it also suggests that for students in greatest need of vocabulary development, additional support is required for them to learn new words. Fisher, Flood, Lapp, & Frey (2004) identified several styles of reading and concluded that interactive styles of reading in which students were actively engaged are more effective than performance or verbatim styles of reading. Read-alouds become interactive when students participate in the reading by such behaviors as answering questions, chiming in

Using Read-Alouds to Teach Vocabulary © 2011 by Karen J. Kindle, Scholastic Teaching Resources

on repetitive text, pointing or labeling, or through movement. In contrast, in performance and verbatim styles of read-alouds students act as the audience, taking a more passive role in the experience. For students most in need of vocabulary development, incorporating simple strategies into the reading supports additional word learning (Biemiller & Boote, 2006). It is important to be selective as you do this, so that the reading of the text does not get so bogged down that students lose the sense of story.

As you read aloud to your students, there are several strategies that you can use to help them learn new words. These include labeling, synonyms, imagery, definitions, examples, context, questioning, clarification, and extension.

Labeling ::

Labeling is one of the strategies that most teachers just seem to incorporate naturally. It is simply a matter of pointing to the illustration as you name the item. It can be done while you read the text or by adding a quick sentence that calls children's attention directly to the item in question. The following examples demonstrate how labeling might be used in reading *Inside Mouse, Outside Mouse* (George, 2004).

Teacher: (*reading text*) "Under the bush, next to the hare." (*points to each item as it is named*)

or

Teacher: (*after reading text*) This is a bush. This is a hare. (*pointing to each item as it is named*)

A variation that makes this strategy interactive is to ask students to locate an item in the illustration. This type of labeling is best used when the teacher is fairly confident that most of the students will be successful.

Reverse labeling involves a slightly different process that again is best used when the teacher is sure that the word is familiar to students. This is a good strategy to use on second or third readings. In reverse labeling, the teacher points to the item and asks the students to name it.

Teacher: (*pointing to the hose*) What is this?

Synonyms ::

In many cases, the target word represents a new word for a familiar concept. At these times, simply providing a synonym works very well. For example, when reading *Snowmen at Night* (Buehner, 2002), you might be concerned that your students would not know the word *cocoa*, so you might insert a synonym or add an extra sentence with a synonym.

Teacher: (*reading text*) "Sipping cups of ice-cold cocoa"—that's chocolate milk—"made by snowman mothers."

or

> **Teacher:** (*after reading page*) See how they look like they are laughing? They are giggling. They're laughing.

Imagery ::

Imagery can be a powerful way of communicating word meaning without interrupting the flow of the story. Imagery can be conveyed through facial expressions or movement. It provides the essence of word meaning, helping children make those initial links that are accomplished through fast mapping (Carey, 1978). Imagery of this type works best when the target words are verbs or convey emotions that can be captured with facial expressions.

The following exchange from *The Three Little Wolves and the Big Bad Pig* (Trivizas, 1993) shows a simple example:

> **Teacher:** (*reading text*) "The pig knocked on the door (*raps knuckles on the desk*) and grunted."

As this example shows, many instances of imagery are just part of what teachers do naturally to create a dramatic reading and sustain students' interest. Look for places to demonstrate word meanings each time you read aloud. It will quickly become a natural part of your practice and support your students in learning novel words.

Imagery can also be used to provide additional context clues. In the following example, the teacher nods her head, a familiar indication of approval, to help students understand what is meant by the word *certainly*.

> **Teacher:** (*reading text*) "'Certainly,' (*nodding head*) said the kangaroo, and she gave them lots of red and yellow bricks."

Another phrase in the story—"*by the hair on our chinny-chin-chins*"—can be reinforced by stroking your chin as you read. While most students are familiar with the story, your ELLs might not know what a chin is.

Definitions ::

One of the simplest strategies for developing vocabulary is to provide an easy-to-understand definition. The challenge is to come up with a definition that provides enough information for your students to understand the story, but not so much that it detracts from the reading. More extensive explanations are better handled during prereading or after-reading discussions. When providing a definition, the teacher can insert the definition either right after reading the word or at the end of the page. An example of each format is provided from *Pumpkin, Pumpkin* (Titherington, 1986).

Using Read-Alouds to Teach Vocabulary © 2011 by Karen J. Kindle, Scholastic Teaching Resources

Teacher: (*reading text*) "Then Jamie scooped out the pumpkin pulp, carved a pumpkin face, and put it in the window." *Carved* means cut. He cut a pumpkin face.

or

Teacher: (*reading text*) "Then Jamie scooped out the pumpkin pulp, carved"— that means *cut*—"a pumpkin face, and put it in the window."

Examples ::

This strategy takes a little more time, so you will probably use it more often before or after reading rather than during reading. Providing examples helps clarify definitions that have been given during the read-aloud. If you have defined a *holiday* as a day that honors an event or person, you might provide Presidents' Day, Thanksgiving, or Mother's Day as examples. Asking students to provide examples is a more difficult task because it requires them to understand the definition and to have sufficient background knowledge to relate to the definition. A student who does not understand what it means to honor someone, or does not celebrate certain holidays, will find it hard to generate examples.

In the following examples from *Welcome to the Ice House* (Yolen, 1998), the teacher would have provided some information about the target words *antler* and *tusk* during reading. In the case of *antler*, the teacher may have used the labeling strategy, pointing to the moose's large rack. The meaning could be reinforced on a later page depicting caribou. Following the reading, the teacher might provide additional examples.

Teacher: (*showing the pictures again*) We see the moose's antlers in this picture, and the caribou's antlers in this picture. These remind me of other animals I have seen that have antlers. We have lots of deer in the woods near my house, and they have antlers like this. I also remember seeing antlers on the reindeer in one of my favorite Christmas books.

or

Teacher: (*showing the illustration of the walrus*) When we were reading, I said that these tusks (*pointing to the tusks*) are special long teeth. It says here that the walrus uses its tusks for defense—to protect itself. Can you think of another animal that has tusks? Are there other animals that have special body parts they use to defend themselves?

Context ::

The use of context clues to determine the meaning of new words is a familiar strategy to most teachers. When using this strategy, we demonstrate how to look for clues to unlock word meaning in the surrounding text. It is important to make your thinking process transparent to students so they learn a strategy that will help them in their independent reading. In the following example, also taken from *Welcome to the Ice House*, the teacher models looking for clues about the meaning of the word *ptarmigan*, using text and picture clues. The illustration shows four wolves atop a snow bank with a hare and a ptarmigan below.

Teacher: (*reading text*) "Or the howling wolfpack sniffing out the track of snowshoe hare or ptarmigan white as wintertide." Hmmm, I know that a hare is a rabbit, but I am not sure what a ptarmigan is. I am going to read this again and look for clues. It says that the wolves are sniffing their tracks, so I think the ptarmigan must be an animal too. When I look at the illustration, I can see the hare right here. Do you see any other animals in the picture? You're right. There is a small, white bird over here. I am thinking that this is probably the ptarmigan.

Once students understand the process from your modeling, you can include them in the process.

Questioning ::

Questioning is one of the most commonly used strategies. We all use this, almost automatically. As we read and come to a word we are not sure the students understand, we simply ask.

Teacher: (*reading from* Mapping Penny's World *[Leedy, 2000]*) "My name is Lisa, and my class is making maps this month." What is a map?

Mary: It shows you where things are.

One problem with this strategy is that it doesn't really tell you much. If one child can respond with a good definition, it doesn't guarantee that other students know the word. The biggest problem with this strategy, however, is that it often results in lots of guessing. Even though the teacher usually ends up providing the definition, students may have heard three or four incorrect guesses—and unfortunately those are the things they sometimes remember. This strategy is best used when you think that most of your students will know the answer.

Clarification ::

This strategy is often used after questioning to clarify a student's response. Especially when dealing with young students, we can expect their initial understandings of words to be incomplete or only partially correct. In these cases, it is important to provide clarification so that misunderstandings can be corrected and a more complete understanding of word meaning can be achieved. In this example, the teacher honors the child's partial understanding of the word *lantern*, but also provides needed clarification.

 Using Read-Alouds to Teach Vocabulary © 2011 by Karen J. Kindle, Scholastic Teaching Resources

Teacher:	(*after reading a page from* Stone Soup *[Muth, 2003]*) They lit lanterns. What are lanterns?
Child:	These lights. (*pointing to the illustration*)
Teacher:	Yes, these are lanterns. They aren't electric, like our lights. You have to light the candle inside for them to light up.

Extension ::

When target words present important concepts, it is often important to provide extensions to further develop understanding. For example, after reading *Gobble it Up!* (Arnosky, 2008), you might want to extend the concept that animals need to live where they can find food.

Teacher:	*Rare* means that something is unusual or not so common. Bamboo is rare, and pandas live in places where bamboo grows. There are other animals like that too. Koala bears only live in Australia. They eat a plant called eucalyptus there that is rare, too.

After Reading: Infusion Activities

Once you have drawn students' attention to a new word during the reading, plan opportunities to use those words in activities again. The amount of attention you give to a single word will depend on its utility, how it fits in your curriculum, and other considerations. More information and examples of these activities can be found in *Teaching Vocabulary in the K–2 Classroom: Easy Strategies for Infusing Vocabulary Learning Into Morning Meetings, Transitions, Centers, and More* (Kindle, 2008). The strategies described below incorporate vocabulary into many daily routines, such as morning board work, journal writing, recess, and even lunchtime.

Categories ::

When students sort words into categories, they are actively engaged in identifying relationships among words and finding connections between new words and words in their existing semantic networks, an essential component of learning new words (Blachowicz & Fisher, 2000). Well-designed categorization activities provide students with countless opportunities for problem solving and flexible, critical thinking.

Categorization can be done on the board, where students identify the "odd man out" from a group of words, or in a pocket chart, where word cards are placed into groups. In either case, it is important to get students to explain their thinking (Durso & Coggins, 1991). This process not only helps develop expressive language skills, but it also often enriches the discussion by presenting a way of looking at things that is "out of the box" and perhaps hadn't even occurred to you!

> Which word doesn't belong?
>
> Christmas, Friday, Columbus Day, Halloween
>
> Tell me why you made your choice.

Sorts that are placed in a pocket chart or center can extend a categorization problem provided during morning board work. For example, you might have students group a list of animals by the number of legs they have, and then use the same list to group by size in a subsequent activity. In a morning Odd Man Out activity, a dolphin might not belong with the leopard shark, queen angel fish, and ray, because it is a mammal, but in the afternoon those same four animals might be correctly grouped together as "animals that live in the ocean." You can try closed sorts in which you determine the categories or criteria for grouping, or you can try the more challenging open sorts in which the students create their own system for classification.

Open Sort	Closed Sort
Put these ocean animals into groups. Explain how each group goes together.	Put the ocean animals into the following groups:
	Animals with hard shells
	Animals with fins
anemone, barnacle, crab, dolphin, eel, whale, jellyfish, shark, octopus, stingray, starfish	*anemone, barnacle, crab, dolphin, eel, whale, jellyfish, shark, octopus, stingray, starfish*

Analogies ::

Analogies help students focus on the relationships between words and ideas (Huff-Benkoski & Greenwood, 1995). The ability to recognize relationships facilitates comprehension and helps students recognize organizational features in text. The following is a list of typical relationships seen in analogies (Smith, 2007), along with an example of each:

Using Read-Alouds to Teach Vocabulary © 2011 by Karen J. Kindle, Scholastic Teaching Resources

1. whole: part (arm: boy; wing: _____)
2. synonyms (crown: tiara; great: _____)
3. antonyms (over: under; above: _____)
4. function, use, or purpose (pencil: write; broom: _____)
5. classification (penguin: bird; dolphin: _____)
6. characteristics and descriptions (whale: large; plankton: _____)
7. degree (drizzle: rain; breeze: _____)
8. cause and effect (heat: burn; cold: _____)

Analogies take a bit more scaffolding than some of the other activities described before your students can solve them independently, but I think you will the extra effort worthwhile.

Line It Up ::

Line It Up is an activity that provides additional exposure for target vocabulary words in a game-like format that promotes flexible and critical thinking. This activity will quickly become a class favorite and can be played every day with new clues.

- **Day 1:** Select 5–7 words that you discussed during your read-aloud. Have the students write the words on index cards. Use this opportunity to remind them of the meanings of the words and call attention to distinctive spelling patterns or phonological features. These cards are stored in a plastic bag or card holder that students keep in their desks.

- **Day 2:** Provide meaning clues. Students mix up their word cards from Day 1 and place them in a row along the top of their desks. As you provide clues, students slide the appropriate cards down. For example, if the word is *content*, you might say, "In the first position, place the word that means 'to be pleased or satisfied.'" Continue until all the cards have been placed. Check by having a student call off the words in order, and review the meaning clues to verify. I like to have my own set of cards that I can place in the pocket chart to provide additional support for my students.

- **Days 3–5:** Play the game with different types of clues. For example, one day you might focus on synonyms or antonyms. Another day, you might focus on phonological or spelling aspects of the words.

Each time you play the game, students hear the words and think about their meanings. You can easily reinforce word meaning at every stage, even when the focus has been phonological. As you confirm a response, it is easy to provide a quick definition, or to ask the student for one. For example, if the clue asked for the word that rhymes with the nonsense word *panky*, and the student correctly placed the word *hanky* in line, you could then respond as follows:

Teacher: Yes, *hanky* rhymes with *panky*. And what is a *hanky*?

Sample Line-It-Up Scripts
for *Hansel and Gretel* (Marshall, 1990)

- **Day 1:** Prepare word cards for the following words: *vast, cottage, famine, ferocious, miserable, lag*. Discuss the meanings of the words, and call students' attention to features such as the number of syllables, the two sounds of *g*, silent-*e* words that "break the rule," and other features as appropriate.

- **Day 2:** Have students place their cards along the top of their desks. As you give the clues, have students pull down the cards to put in position. Day 2 clues focus on meaning. Here are some sample clues:

  - *In the first place, put the card that means "a little house."*
  - *In the second place, put the word that means "to fall behind."*
  - *The third word means that something is big and spread out.*
  - *The next word means "a time when there isn't enough food for people to eat."*
  - *In the next place, put the word that means you are really, really unhappy.*
  - *The last word means that something is fierce or wild.*

- **Day 3:** Focus on the phonological or spelling aspects of the words. Here are some sample clues:

  - *The first word has four syllables.*
  - *The next word has the /sh/ sound in the middle.*
  - *This word has the hard sound of* g.
  - *The next word has the soft sound of* g.
  - *This word has a silent* e, *but it doesn't have a long vowel sound.*
  - *This word rhymes with* mast.

Clothesline ::

This activity has many variations published in the literature. This version is most closely related to word chains (Tompkins, 2006). Some lists of words that you select from your read-aloud lend themselves to comparison or sequencing. In comparisons, students place words in order by specific criteria, such as size or degree. For example, after reading *Biggest, Strongest, Fastest* (Jenkins, 1995), you might have students place the animals in the book,

Using Read-Alouds to Teach Vocabulary © 2011 by Karen J. Kindle, Scholastic Teaching Resources

such as elephant, cheetah, shrew, and flea, in order from largest to smallest. Some groups of words will be perfect for time sequencing. After reading *Pumpkin, Pumpkin* (Titherington, 1986) or *It's Pumpkin Time!* (Hall, 1994), students can sequence words such as *seed, sprout, bud, flower,* and *pumpkin* on teacher-created cards.

After you have selected the words for the activity, have students come up and hold the word cards, discussing them briefly as you hand them out. Students stand in front of the room with the card visible to the class. For younger students and ELLs, adding a picture clue provides additional support. Call on the rest of the class to help you arrange the students in order, providing clues as needed.

Teacher: If we want to place these animals in order from largest to smallest, which one would come first?

or

Teacher: Now that we have the largest and smallest animals sorted out, where would you put the shrew? Remember our book said that the shrew is about two or three inches long.

Clothesline activities are so named because I actually had a clothesline (made of yarn) hung in a corner of my room. Once the class has worked through a set, the word cards are put in a basket along with the clothespins. You can use regular wooden clothespins or find clothespin-shaped paper clips at an office supply store. Students use the clothespins to fasten the cards on the line in a particular order. The activity can easily be modified by changing the criteria. For example, after students have placed the animals in order from largest to smallest, you can ask them to think about how they would order them from fastest to slowest. There isn't always a right answer, but the discussions that result from disagreements really support word learning and deep thinking. Students can record their work by writing the words on paper in the order they were placed on the clothesline. This provides a means of monitoring their understanding of target terms.

An advantage of this activity is that the card sets can be kept in a center and reviewed on a regular basis so students don't forget the words. Additional cards can be added to sets as you encounter the words in other texts, but keep the total number of cards to about 10.

Act It Out ::

We are all familiar with charades. Students enjoy the opportunity to get up and move around, and some words can be *shown* more easily than they can be explained or described. If the words you have selected for your read-aloud focus lend themselves to imagery, this is a great way to provide vocabulary reinforcement during transition times, such as before lunch, or waiting for the dismissal bell. Act It Out can be used in a variety of ways. You can call a word, such as *wiggle* or *pout,* and have one or more students perform the action or you can have a single child act it out for other students to guess.

Picture It ::

This activity helps students learn word meanings by associating the word with a visual image. The picture might be a depiction of the word meaning—for example, a sketch of a flamingo—but it may also present the word in a more abstract way. Your computer will give you countless ways to play with fonts to create word images. Here are some examples:

   s — t — r — e — t — c — h

Phonological and Phonemic Awareness and Phonics ::

Activities that help primary students with phonological and phonemic awareness and decoding skills are important to include in any early literacy classroom. It is not difficult to take these components, which you are already are using on a daily basis, and infuse your target vocabulary words into them for additional exposures.

Bingo. Bingo games are always popular with young students, and they can be easily adapted to provide practice with skills and develop vocabulary at the same time. The example presented here focuses on phonemic awareness, but you could just as easily make your clues deal with word meanings. Be sure you always give information about the word in your clues. For example, instead of just saying "/h/—humpback," add a little information using the text context by saying,"/h/— humpbacks leap: humpback whales leap high out of the waves and come splashing down" (from *Into the A, B, Sea* by Deborah Lee Rose; see Chapter 5). As an alternative to using bingo cards and distributing markers to cover spaces, I often use the sets of plastic letters (or you could use letter cards) from making-words activities with my class. Each child picks five letters from his or her bag and lines them up on the desk. When the sound representing a letter is called, students slide that plastic letter or letter card down until all five letters are at the bottom of the desk—and that is their bingo!

Making words. Many primary teachers routinely schedule making-words activities into their lesson plans. Developed by Cunningham (2000), this hands-on activity helps children develop the alphabetic principle and phonics skills in a very concrete manner. In making-words activities, students are given a predetermined set of letters. They begin by constructing a familiar two- or three-letter word and are prompted to add or remove letters to make new and more complex words. The activity concludes with students using all the letters to construct the mystery word. Try selecting one key word from your read-aloud list as the mystery word and build your making-words lesson from that. Although your focus will be on spelling patterns and understanding how words work, look for opportunities to mix in new and interesting words and/or to review past words that might fit the patterns you are teaching.

Word sorts and spelling. Chances are that some of the words you select for instruction during your read-alouds will be examples of the spelling patterns you are teaching, either in a more traditional weekly list or through developmental spelling and word sorts. Keep track of the words you teach during read-alouds and then revisit them as you teach applicable spelling patterns. For example, this week you might be reading *In the Small, Small Pond* (Fleming, 1993) and introducing the words *tug* and *lug*. Next week, those same words might appear on a spelling list of short *u* words; or be included in a word sort of short- and long-*u* words.

Writing ::

One of the most exciting things to me as a teacher is reading my students' independent writing and seeing how they have infused vocabulary into their work. When they begin to experiment with incorporating new words into their written expression, you can be fairly confident that these words have a home in their lexicon. For some students, words will pop up spontaneously; for others you will need to provide some scaffolded support. Young children often begin their writing with drawing and/or expressing their ideas verbally (Rog, 2007). As you encourage your students to use target vocabulary in prewriting conversations, you are providing support for their use of these words.

Students who feel less confident in their writing abilities, and our ELL students often are in this group, feel safer when sticking to a familiar pattern in their writing. Even if you provide a word bank with animal names, you are likely to get writing such as the sentences shown below when you ask these students to write about their favorite animal from the story:

- *I like the elephant.*

- *I like the cheetah.*

Your goal is to help your students feel comfortable taking some risks. They should be encouraged to use the target terms in writing as much as possible. This can be accomplished in a variety of ways.

Modeling. As you model good writing to your students, show them how you deliberately incorporate target words into your writing.

Teacher: Boys and girls, I want to write about how I planted my garden at home. I am thinking that there are some words we read in *It's Pumpkin Time!* that might help me. We read about seeds, and I planted seeds. I had to make holes in the dirt. Our book uses the words *shovel* and *soil*. That makes my sentence sound better: I used my shovel to plant the seeds in the soil.

Journal writing. As you conference with students about their own writing, you can prompt them to add target terms. Be sure to call everyone's attention to the use of these words during share time.

Morning message. If you do a morning message in your class, this is a great way to show your students how the target vocabulary can be used in other contexts. You may highlight an alternate meaning of the word, show how it is used in figurative language, or set it up in a context that points out shades of meaning.

Writing center. Students need lots of time to write independently. A writing center is a standard feature in many primary classrooms that provides students with the opportunity to practice and solidify newly acquired skills, and also to experiment with language. Your read-aloud books can be placed in the writing center as a prompt for work that will include target vocabulary. You can ask students to respond in a variety of ways: writing captions for illustrations, describing things they see in the illustrations, writing about a favorite or interesting aspect of the book—the possibilities are endless.

Content writing. The ability to produce nonfiction texts is important at younger and younger ages. Diagrams, charts, and tables are ways that ELLs and other students who struggle with language can represent what they have learned. Science and math journals are becoming more common as young children learn to write about the processes they use to solve problems as well as to document their observations.

When your read-aloud is a piece of expository text, the form of the text will often give you inspiration. For example, *Tadpole Diary* (Drew, 1997) presents information about the life cycle of frogs in a journal format as though written by students making and recording their observations. There are diagrams, tables, and charts that show students different ways of organizing information. If you have read several books about frogs, helping your students amass that information in one of these formats will provide them with additional exposures to key vocabulary terms as they use the terms for authentic purposes.

Math ::

Target vocabulary can easily be infused into a number of mathematical strands by incorporating the words into word problems and other math activities.

Operations. If you read a book with animal names for example, it is a simple matter to build those words into your problems for addition and subtraction, for example:

Teacher: Five humpback whales were swimming along in the ocean. Three leapt out of the water. How many were left in the ocean?

or

Teacher: The hungry leopard shark ate two queen angel fish and four flying fish. How many fish did the leopard shark eat in all?

Encourage your students to write their own word problems by keeping words in a word bank or on a chart where everyone has access to them.

Measurement. Some nonfiction read-alouds lend themselves perfectly to reinforcing measurement concepts. Books such as *Biggest, Strongest, Fastest* and *Hottest, Coldest,*

Highest, Deepest, both by Steve Jenkins, will provide you with many opportunities to incorporate vocabulary into your math lessons.

Teacher: We learned that the tiny flea can jump eight inches in the air. Use your inch ruler and draw a line that is eight inches long.

or

Teacher: The bee hummingbird is the smallest bird—it is only three inches long. Draw a bird on your paper that is longer than the bee hummingbird and measure it with your inch ruler.

Patterns. Other math skills that can be infused with vocabulary include patterns and graphing. Pattern games can be constructed with more than colors and letters. Try having your students develop ABC patterns using words from your read-alouds.

Teacher: Anemone, barnacle, crab, anemone, barnacle, crab . . .

Graphing. You can have your students create graphs that include the vocabulary words in many cases. After reading a book with unusual animals, you can make a graph that depicts class favorites. Be sure to have each student explain why the animal is his or her favorite in order to give him or her a chance to use the animal name in authentic oral language. It is a good opportunity to add in little extra bits of information about the animals as well.

Teacher: Susan, you said that the zebra is your favorite because it has stripes. Did you know that the stripes on zebras are all a little bit different and they can be brown as well as black?

Music ::

Young children enjoy singing. The rhythm and rhyme of children's songs develop phonological awareness, and many times, the melody and lyrics can serve as a memory aid. Almost every child will sing the alphabet song if you ask them to tell you their letters. My own children could rattle off the names of the fifty states in alphabetical order—but only by singing the song, of course.

Piggyback songs are created by putting new words to familiar tunes. It can be a bit challenging to come up with new lyrics that incorporate your target vocabulary while maintaining the rhythm and rhyme scheme of the original, but your music teacher might be willing to help you with this. I think you will find that once you have created a few, it gets easier each time.

Songs are a great way to infuse vocabulary because they can be sung over and over again. If you are able to add movement of some kind, word meaning is reinforced each time students sing the song. Music makes a great transition activity as well, ensuring that instructional content is packed into every possible minute of the day.

Science/Social Studies ::

Many times, you will select a nonfiction text to read aloud because it supports your curricular objectives. For example, you might be studying weather or animal homes and make your text selections to enhance or extend your lessons. At other times, you will select nonfiction read-alouds based on student interests. You might find that you have a group of first graders who are particularly interested in dinosaurs. Your kindergartners might be fascinated with construction vehicles when they observe road work in front of the school.

Content area words often require more instruction than you can effectively deal with during the course of a read-aloud. These words often represent both new words and new concepts, identified by Graves (2006) as the most difficult word meanings to acquire. During your read-aloud, you will want to provide your initial instruction on the new word or term, but then follow up in your science or social studies time or in centers with additional activities that really solidify meaning for your students.

Activities that help make the abstract concepts more concrete will help your students immensely. Visualization strategies, such as using graphic organizers and manipulatives, can help here. Think beyond Venn diagrams and Unifix cubes when you are thinking of manipulatives. Additionally, activities that help your students understand relationships between words will be helpful to incorporate.

Concept circles (Harmon, Wood, & Hedrick, 2006) are easy to use and provide a visual means of the categorization exercises mentioned earlier. For example, if you are studying plants, you might read *It's Pumpkin Time!* (Hall, 1994). As you read, you identify the words describing plant parts as being important and use the labeling strategy. To provide additional instruction, you use a concept circle. Students must determine which term does not belong in the circle. You can provide the category—in this case, plant parts—for students, or let them identify the category on their own.

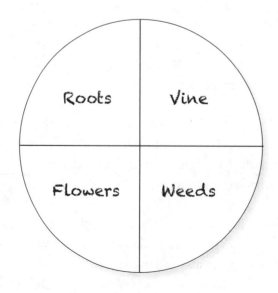

Using Read-Alouds to Teach Vocabulary © 2011 by Karen J. Kindle, Scholastic Teaching Resources

Another way of providing additional exposure to the same target vocabulary is to construct a Build a Plant activity, based on Build a Cowboy (Kindle, 2008). Make a large drawing of a plant with the parts you want to discuss clearly depicted and then cut the drawing apart so that each plant part is a separate piece. Each day, you add a piece or two, naming the part and discussing its function. By the end of the week, you will have a diagram of the entire plant with the parts clearly labeled.

Activities such as these provide additional exposure to the words you selected for instruction during your read-alouds and give the additional information your students will need to really get hold of these concepts.

Recess ::

Recess seems to be an odd time to be thinking about vocabulary development, but there are many opportunities to infuse your target words in both informal conversation with students and in structured activities. It is easy to ask a student whether he or she sees cirrus or cumulus clouds in the sky or to comment on the shape of the leaves on the flower a child has picked for you.

Outdoor games can often be adapted to include interesting verbs. Games such as Mother May I? and relay races can be infused with your target words so that students get to experience the movement—not just hear the word. For example, in a relay race, you could ask your students to run up to the line, *twirl* the hula hoop three times, and run back. Always be sure to remind them of the meaning, both verbally and with your own demonstration.

Cafeteria ::

Another opportunity to infuse vocabulary instruction can be found in the cafeteria. All it takes is a little creativity and a watchful eye for the teachable moment. If your target list from a read-aloud contains texture words (*creamy, fluffy, crisp*), color words, flavor words, aroma words, or other descriptors, you may be able to find a way to work the words into a comment to a child about his or her lunch.

An advantage to this setting is that it will provide you with ways to show alternate meanings or varied contexts in which a word might be used. For example, while reading *It's Pumpkin Time!* (Hall, 1994), suppose you showed students the picture of the shovel being used to plant the seeds. At lunch, you might comment how their spoon is like a shovel when it dips into the pudding, or talk about the expression "shoveling it in" to describe someone who is eating very fast. If you are talking about plants, you can show your students that the celery stalks they are eating are the plant stems and that carrots are roots.

In Chapter 4, you will see a framework for incorporating these before, during, and after reading strategies to create a vocabulary unit based on a read-aloud.

Constructing Vocabulary Units Based on Read-Alouds

Effective read-alouds that support vocabulary development do not just happen—they are carefully planned. It is best to select five or six key words because too many words interrupt the flow of the story and the read-aloud loses its benefits. As you begin to plan, I recommend scripting definitions and comments on sticky notes so that you will not hesitate during the reading. I still do that when I model the process to teachers and my students. After you have read the story a few times, the process becomes more natural and vocabulary instruction is woven into the reading in such a way that it becomes part of the fabric of the read-aloud.

When developing a unit, it is important to keep a few things in mind. Neuman & Dwyer (2009) identified five principles of effective vocabulary instruction that they used in a study evaluating published reading programs. Although this study was focused on preschool programs, the principles are applicable to the primary grades and read-alouds as well.

1. Words to be taught and learned should be identified in advance. Without this prior planning, it is easy to focus on too many words and lose the sense of story.

2. Specific strategies for teaching those words should be determined. The teacher must decide if labeling will provide sufficient word knowledge or if examples are also needed.

3. Opportunities for students to use the words in context should be structured.

4. Previously learned words should be reviewed with students.

5. Teachers must have a plan for monitoring learning. Activities should be planned that provide evidence of students' satisfactory understanding of the target terms.

Designing a Vocabulary Unit Based on a Read-Aloud

The following steps are meant to serve as a template for unit construction. By sharing the process with you, I hope that you will feel equipped to create your own units. Vocabulary units in this context consist of the read-aloud (one or multiple readings) and the subsequent infusion activities that you structure to provide those critical additional exposures. Units may be based on a single text, multiple texts by a single author, multiple texts on a topic, or companion texts (fiction and nonfiction). Units may vary in length from one day to several weeks.

1. **Select the text for your read-aloud:** It all starts with the text.

   a. *Choose texts with illustrations that are large enough to be seen by the entire class.* Big books are a great option, but limiting yourself to big books will rule out many excellent choices. The next best option is to select books that have large, simple illustrations and cluster your students around you so they can see.

   b. *Consider the length of the text.* Shorter books can be read multiple times without a significant investment of time. It is difficult for some students to maintain their attention if books are too long. If you find a wonderful book that seems too long, however, you can always break it up into several readings.

   c. *Consider the language of the text.* Texts with rhythm and rhyme sustain students' interest through multiple readings. Narrative texts such as fairy tales help children who have not had as many experiences with literacy develop an understanding of story grammars.

   d. *Select a text with vocabulary in mind.* While students' books on average contain more rare words than adult conversation (Hayes & Ahrens, 1988) some books have more than others. Look for words that are unusual, interesting, or just plain fun to say. How many of us still remember *supercalifragilisticexpialidocious* just because it was so much fun to say!

2. **Analyze the vocabulary in the text:** The next step in the process is to analyze the text to identify the words you will target for instruction. There are usually more words than you could possibly use, so it is important to make good decisions. As you read the text, place words into three groups.

   a. *Group 1: Words that students are likely to be familiar with.* Note that even very common words might not be familiar to ELLs, so it is important to know your learners. An example might be a word such as *cement*. While most of my students might know this word, I might need to point out the cement on the playground to my ELLs to help them understand what the word means.

b. *Group 2: Words that represent new terms for familiar concepts or new concepts for familiar words.* As an example of a new term for a familiar concept, your students might not be familiar with the term *cement*, but very familiar with the term *concrete*. This can occur when students move to your classroom from different parts of the country and the terms they use are different from the norm in your area.

c. *Group 3: Words that represent new terms and new concepts.* These words require the most instruction since both the term and the concept represent new learning.

3. **Narrow down the list of vocabulary to five to seven words:** Select the words you want to focus on for instruction. You might select some words because of their importance to your curricular content, some words because they are highly useful, some because they are examples of morphemes, and others because they are just fun. There really aren't any wrong choices—but over time you will get more skilled at selecting the best words. If you have difficulty narrowing down the list, you can always extend your unit and add more words.

4. **Plan your read-aloud:** Once you have selected the words you want to target, you are ready to plan your read-aloud. Decide whether you will be reading the text one time only or if this text can sustain multiple readings. Determine which of the strategies described in Chapter 3 seem best suited for developing the vocabulary. For example, if the word is depicted clearly in an illustration, labeling might be the best strategy to choose. For an action word, visual imagery might work well. Will a simple synonym be enough or should you provide a short definition? Are you going to use questioning strategies or will you provide the information to the students? Your instructional decisions should be based on the specific word, the context in which it appears, and your word learning goals. Also, consider the timing of your instruction. Some words can be dealt with very effectively in the context of a picture walk before reading. For other words, particularly for those representing new words and new concepts, you may want to provide a definition during reading, and follow up with clarification or examples *after* reading.

5. **Design infusion activities:** After you have planned the read-aloud, think about the ways that you can infuse the target words into your daily instructional routines and interactions with your students. The nature of the words you select will guide you. Some lists are perfectly suited to sorting and classification activities, while others might work best for outdoor activities. You should not only incorporate infusion activities daily for the length of the unit, but also revisit important words and concepts throughout the year.

Using Read-Alouds to Teach Vocabulary © 2011 by Karen J. Kindle, Scholastic Teaching Resources

Application: A Sample Unit Construction

The following sample unit is based on the book *When Winter Comes* (Van Laan, 2000) and was part of a curricular unit on the seasons. It provides an example of how the steps described above were put into action.

Select the Text ::

When Winter Comes was selected for several reasons. First, the content supported curricular objectives by showing how seasons change and how different animals adapt to those changes. In addition, the text has simple organization in its question-and-answer language pattern. The illustrations are large enough to be seen by the whole class, and the text is short and engaging enough to sustain multiple reads. The rhythm and rhyme are appealing and provide opportunities to support other literacy objectives. Most important, this simple text is packed full of rich, vivid vocabulary and figurative language. Despite the high density of unfamiliar words in this book, the context is supportive with its repetitive structure and the presence of familiar animals and natural occurrences.

Analyze the Vocabulary ::

In analyzing the vocabulary for this text, I limited consideration to nouns, verbs, adjectives, and adverbs since they are critical for comprehension in this text. Since the text uses imagery, words are often used metaphorically, and thus are included in Group 2 when at first glance they might seem better placed in Group 1. My grouping for the words follows:

- Group 1: *leaves, winter, winds, snow, ground, flowers, seeds, caterpillars, wound, waiting, spring, soft, warm-weather, sun, field mice, deer, fish, pond, dark, quietly*

- Group 2: *blow, tumble, blanket, bed, wilt, rest, golden, crown, songbirds, bask, mossy, tunnel, nest, dappled, icebound, circle, snuggling*

- Group 3: *petals, burrow, cocoons, south, thistledown, wander, knit, mound, gust*

Groupings are tentative. You may find that a word you placed in group 3 is really familiar to your students or that a word you assumed they knew is unfamiliar.

Narrow Down the List ::

One glance at the lists above makes it obvious why we have to narrow down the list for target vocabulary. Trying to provide instruction on all of these words would ruin the flow of the reading and totally obliterate the sound of the language, which is such an integral part of this text. For focused instruction, I selected *south, burrow, tunnel, icebound, gust, seeds, tumble,* and *wilt.* These choices were affected by several factors. Since I was tying this text to my science instruction, I included words that focused on animals' adaptations to the approach of winter and related concepts that my students, living in a southern state, would need more support to understand. Since there were several other read-alouds that were part of this unit, this text was only going to be read two or three times, so focusing on too many words was not possible. That said, there are many ways to continue to cover many more words in your infusion activities than you can within the read-aloud itself, as you will see on pages 39–42.

Plan the Read-Aloud ::

The plan provided here describes how you might plan your instruction when you are doing multiple readings over multiple days. The plan would of course be adapted if you were considering a single reading. It is helpful to keep in mind that your instruction can occur before, during, or after reading—or any combination. In the following example, I planned a detailed picture walk, so a short introduction seemed appropriate.

Teacher: Today we are going to read a story about what happens when winter comes. What do you think happens when winter comes? What animals do you think we might find in this book? Let's take a picture walk and see if we are right.

As we looked at the illustrations, I used labeling strategies to identify the animals and other items that the students might not know.

- *Look at these **flowers***. *What do you notice about their **petals**?*
- *This is a **cocoon**. The **caterpillar** is inside.*
- *See how the **field mice** are down in the **tunnel**?*

After the picture walk, I read the entire story without interruptions so that students could experience the language of the story.

The next day, during the second reading of the text, I focused on elaboration of word meanings. I found ways to use visual imagery in the format of simple gestures or facial expressions. For example, while reading *tumble*, I traced the leaves' movements down the page with my finger. I provided brief, easy-to-understand definitions.

Teacher: Their petals wilt. That means they dry up, like you see here in the picture.

The number of words you want to highlight and the number of times you plan to read the text will help you decide how many words to elaborate in a given reading. It is important to always maintain a good balance between the read-aloud and instruction. During subsequent readings, you can vary the focus of instruction to different words or different aspects of the words. For example you might want to emphasize the rhyme patterns.

Teacher: "Where oh where do caterpillars go when winter comes and the cold winds—"

Students: "Blow!"

Teacher: Show me how you feel when the cold wind blows.

or

Teacher: What part of the words *mound* and *ground* is the same?

You can also cover target words with sticky notes. Students use their knowledge or syntax and semantics to predict what the covered word might be and then revise or confirm their predictions as you reveal the letters one by one. Be sure to always include a comment about word meaning even when the focus of the interaction deals with visual aspects of the word; for example, you might cover the word *tunnel*. Using semantic cues, students might predict the word *dig* will be under the sticky note and revise their prediction as you reveal the initial letters.

Teacher: *Tunnel* is another word for *dig* and is also the name of the hole the mouse digs.

Design Infusion Activities ::

Look at your list of words and begin to find ways where you can infuse them into your daily routines and instruction. It may feel a little forced at first, but you'll find that opportunities start popping up in unexpected places. With a little creativity and ingenuity, it is easy to find occasions to use the target words in fun and engaging ways. Some sample activities for *When Winter Comes* are provided below.

Categories: I wrote target words on cards for sorting activities using the pocket chart. Once the activities were done with the whole class, I placed them in a center for small-group work. The same set of words can be sorted in multiple ways.

- **Day 1:** Sort words by plant or animal.

- **Day 2:** Sort words associated with winter and words for other seasons.

- **Day 3:** Sort words into nouns and verbs.

Odd Man Out: Ask students to identify which word in a group does not belong and to explain why. Having students explain their reasoning is a critical part of this process because it helps you assess their word knowledge. Here are some examples:

- *songbird, deer, field mouse, fish* (fish)

- *wind, snow, ice, spring* (spring)

- *circle, blow, gust, dappled* (dappled)
- *bask, sun, warm-weather, dark* (dark)

For this classification activity, you can either write the words on the board or do the activity orally.

Analogies: I like to use analogies because they foster critical-thinking skills. The particular words from the word set for *When Winter Comes* worked well with analogies focusing on characteristics (animals/movements) and classifications (animals/habitats).

- **Field mouse** is to **burrow** as **fish** is to _____. (**pond**)
- **Fish** is to **pond** as **caterpillar** is to _____. (**cocoon**)
- **Leaf** is to **tumble** as **petal** is to _____. (**wilt**)

Phonological and phonemic awareness: Rhyming activities are an obvious choice for this text and can be done in a variety of ways. Make up sentences that use rhyming words from the text and have students supply the missing words.

- *Field mice tunnel in the ground, and deer snuggle in a _____.* (*mound*)
- *The leaves fall off and tumble down, making a blanket on the _____.* (*ground*)

Generate rhymes from words in the text. They can be real or nonsense words for this activity.

Teacher: Can you think of a word that rhymes with _____?

Beginning sounds bingo: Have your students write one letter in each box of their bingo game board. You can give them a list of letters to choose from or let them choose their own letters. Use the words from the text as your clues, including a sentence that provides a definition, example, or extends word knowledge. Here are some examples:

Teacher: Pond. In the winter the pond becomes icebound and the fish stay underneath the ice. Pond. If you have the letter that you hear at the beginning of the word *pond*, you can cover that space.

Teacher: Dappled. The deer have little white spots on their fur. They are dappled. If you have the letter you hear at the beginning of the word *dappled*, you can cover that space.

Rhyming word bingo: Provide students with a list of words that are easily rhymed. Students select eight words to write on their programmable bingo cards. Your clues should be something like the following:

Using Read-Alouds to Teach Vocabulary © 2011 by Karen J. Kindle, Scholastic Teaching Resources

Teacher: If you have a word that rhymes with **must**, put a marker on that space. (*The student would then cover the target word* **gust**.)

Cafeteria: If you keep your word list in mind when you are on lunch duty in the cafeteria, you may be able to find ways to infuse target vocabulary during typical lunchtime interactions with your students. Here are some examples:

- *That piece of lettuce looks a bit wilted—just like the petals in the story.*

- *If you drop your tray, everything will tumble to the ground.*

- *The wrapper for your straw reminds me a little of the cocoon for the caterpillar.*

Math: It is usually pretty easy to find ways to infuse vocabulary into your math instruction. If you do a word problem each day, you can usually find a way to build in the target vocabulary.

- *There were 5 little fish swimming in the pond. An ice fisherman caught 2 of the fish. How many fish were left?*

- *Three dappled deer were snuggling behind the oak tree. Three more were in a mound behind the bushes. How may dappled deer were there in all?*

If you use multiple problem-solving strategies, such as acting out the problem or drawing pictures to solve, your students will get an additional reinforcement of word meaning.

- *One songbird has 2 wings. Draw a picture to find out how many wings 3 songbirds would have.*

Your specific math objectives will influence your choice of activities. For example, if you were working on estimation or measurement concepts, you might pose the following types of questions:

- *Which would be longer, a caterpillar or a field mouse?*

- *Which would weigh more, a fish or a deer?*

Music: Some people find it easy to make up tunes and write lyrics. I like to use existing tunes that I think my students will be familiar with and then adapt words to fit. For this unit, I used "Oh Where, Oh Where Has My Little Dog Gone?" Sometimes it is easy. Other times, I find it hard to do. Again, the music teacher at your school may be able to help. You can also make song charts or write the words on sentences strips for the pocket chart and use the songs for shared reading activities, for example:

Oh Where, Oh Where

(follow the pattern of the song, substituting the following phrases):

Oh where, oh where, have the leaves all gone? (*hand over eyes, searching*)

Oh where, oh where can they be?

The leaves tumble down (*roll hands*)

And blanket the ground (*spreading motion*)

For winter is coming, you see. (*hug self, shivering*)

Oh where, oh where, have the flowers all gone? (*hand over eyes, searching*)

Oh where, oh where can they be?

Their petals wilt (*shrug down*)

And the seeds burrow down (*burrowing motion*)

For winter is coming, you see.

Oh where, oh where, have the caterpillars all gone? (*hand over eyes, searching*)

Oh where, oh where can they be?

Inside their cocoons, (*hug self tightly*)

So tightly wound

For winter is coming, you see.

Oh where, oh where, have the field mice all gone? (*hand over eyes, searching*)

Oh where, oh where can they be?

Tunneling down (*tunneling motion*)

To their nests underground,

For winter is coming, you see.

Oh where, oh where, have the dappled deer gone? (*hand over eyes, searching*)

Oh where, oh where can they be?

Making no sound (*finger to lips*)

Closely knit in a mound, (*lacing fingers together*)

For winter is coming, you see.

Oh where, oh where, have the fish all gone? (*hand over eyes, searching*)

Oh where, oh where can they be?

In the icebound pond,

They circle around,

For winter is coming, you see.

Using Read-Alouds to Teach Vocabulary © 2011 by Karen J. Kindle, Scholastic Teaching Resources

Developing vocabulary units takes a little time at first, but like anything else, the more you do it, the easier it gets. With a template, or framework, such as the one I have provided in this chapter, you will find that you start generating ideas for activities the very first time you look through a book. As you begin designing units, start with just a few words and focus on the read-aloud portion of the unit. Then select one or two activities that you think will be appropriate for your students, and add them in. Before you know it, you will be infusing rich vocabulary instruction throughout the day!

In the next two chapters, you will find suggestions for read-alouds along with an assortment of infusion activities. Chapter 5 contains nonfiction texts and Chapter 6 contains fiction titles.

Nonfiction Read-Aloud Units

Nonfiction texts used to be a rare sight in primary classrooms (Cash & Schumm, 2006). In a study of first-grade classrooms, Duke (2000) found that only 9.8 percent of the books in classroom libraries were informational and that the total time spent on activities related to nonfiction texts averaged only 3.6 minutes per day. The increase in the availability of quality nonfiction texts that are suitable for young children has increased dramatically in recent years, but teachers may need to make conscious efforts to increase their use of these texts in read-alouds.

The following vocabulary unit plans are designed to get you started. They provide a menu of possibilities that you can use as presented, or adapt to fit the needs of your students and your own unique personality. There is no particular order in most cases. Some activities might be repeated multiple times with some slight variations; others might be done only once or omitted entirely.

The format for the units in this chapter and in Chapter 6, which contains fiction texts, is consistent. Each unit begins with a brief description of the text. In the section titled "Vocabulary for Instruction," you will find a list of potential target words. Additional word lists suggest specific categories that you can focus on, such as "Action words," "Multiple meaning words," and "Miscellaneous." These lists may contain a combination of possible target words and new words. For example, in the Van Laan unit described in the previous chapter (see pages 37–42), you might group words into nouns, verbs, adjectives, and adverbs. These suggested groupings might be helpful to you in narrowing down the word list. You will still need to examine the words and determine whether they fall into Group 1, Group 2, or Group 3 (see Chapter 4, pages 35–36, for an explanation of this process). In most cases, there are many more possible words than you would want to target for instruction.

The next section in each unit, "During Reading," contains suggestions for questions you might incorporate in your reading to promote critical thinking and the use of target vocabulary. Although you are the best judge of which strategies to use for your purposes and to meet the needs of your students, some general suggestions are included to facilitate the selection process.

The final section in each unit, "Infusion Activities," provides you with a variety of possible activities for infusing vocabulary instruction from the read-aloud throughout your day. It is by no means an exhaustive list. You will undoubtedly find additional ways to incorporate your target words into your daily routines.

UNIT 1

Hottest, Coldest, Highest, Deepest by Steve Jenkins

Text description: *Through this text, students learn more about their world. Steve Jenkins guides readers to the hottest, coldest, highest, and deepest places on earth. The text is supported by the author's distinctive style of illustration. This is also a great text for ELL students since it talks about places around the globe.*

Each page contains several features. The main text is quite short—often just one or two sentences. There is an additional inset containing text that provides more details useful in extending the discussion. An inset map shows the featured location, and a world map on the final page shows all the locations discussed in the text.

Other graphics support students in understanding the numbers presented. For example, on the page discussing the hottest place on earth, a diagram shows thermometers that depict room temperature, average body temperature, and the air temperature in the Sahara Desert.

At first glance, the text may seem too difficult to use as a read-aloud, but it is great for introducing the ideas of comparatives and superlatives, so don't immediately rule it out for your young readers. For young children, I would read only the large text on each page—but you can add bits of information provided in the small print as their interests and questions lead you.

Although each page has an inset map showing the highlighted location, the maps are very small and will not be visible to the whole class. This problem can be easily remedied by having a map or globe handy when you read this text so you can be prepared to locate the places discussed. You can even make extensions on subsequent days by having students use the inset map on the page and then locating the spot on the globe.

You may find that the numbers provided are not very meaningful for your students. In that case, you may want to omit those numbers and just focus on the concepts. For example, on the first page of text, you could omit the sentence "It is 4.145 miles long" and just concentrate on the idea or concept of "longest."

Vocabulary for Instruction

This text is packed full of possible target words, particularly if you incorporate words from the insets and items in the illustrations that are not specifically mentioned. For young children, the concepts listed below are useful words for targeted instruction. The vocabulary related to landforms and habitats might be important to target if the words are well matched to your social studies or science curriculum.

Possible target words: *longest, deepest, oldest, highest, hottest, wettest, coldest, driest, windiest, active, extreme, snowiest*

Concepts: *long (longest), deep (deepest), old (oldest), high, hot, cold, wet, dry, windy, active, extreme, snowy*

Opposites: *long/short, old/young, hot/cold, wet/dry, deep/high*

Geography: *river, lake, mountain, desert, rainforest, waterfall, volcano*

Animals: *camel, mountain goat, jellyfish, penguin, tree frog, toucan, viperfish, iguana*

Miscellaneous: *pyramid, peak, palm tree, dune, planet, submarine, tide, vines, erupts*

During Reading

Since many of the words in this text represent concepts, you'll use the definition and examples strategies frequently. Labeling also works well for many words, since the illustrations are large and colorful. Be sure to point out key items that are not specifically mentioned in the text. For example, on the page that talks about the Nile River, you would want to label the camel and pyramids. Be sure to prepare those definitions in advance—it can be difficult to think of how to explain a concept such as "tides" in child-friendly terms on the fly.

Suggestions for questions that serve as extensions and promote critical thinking are provided below, along with some additional ideas to incorporate during or after your reading.

- *How is a **river** different from a stream? From a **lake**?* (questioning/clarification)
- Your students might find interesting the graphic showing that some rivers are actually longer than the United States is wide. Lay a piece of blue yarn on the map to trace a river's route. Then straighten the yarn to show how long the river's path really is. (imagery)

Using Read-Alouds to Teach Vocabulary © 2011 by Karen J. Kindle, Scholastic Teaching Resources

- *This is a very unusual fish. Have you ever seen a fish that looks like this?* (questioning) (Students may notice the bumps on its back and sides; the long, cigar shape; the whiskers, similar to those of a catfish; or the disc behind its eye.) *This fish appears to be the Baikal sturgeon. The barbells (whiskers) are used to help the sturgeon find food. It has plates instead of scales.* (You can find information regarding this fish on the Internet, if you have students who exhibit interest in learning more.)

- *The **peak** is the very top of the mountain—sometimes it's called the summit.* (definition, synonym)

- ***Mount** is a short way to say mountain. Lots of mountains have that name, like Mt. St. Helens, or Mt. McKinley.* (definition)

- *Why aren't there more plants besides the **palm trees** growing here in the **desert**?* (questioning/extension)

- *What makes the sand pile up in these **dunes**?* (questioning/extension)

- ***Penguins** are birds—but they don't fly! How are penguins like other birds, and how are they different? I notice that in this picture, the penguin almost does look like he's flying.* (extension, clarification)

- *How do you think the **penguins** stay warm in the **coldest** place on earth?* (questioning/extension)

- *On this **mountain** in Hawaii, it rains 350 days per year. That means that in the whole year, there would only be 15 days without rain falling.* (extension)

- *Can anything live where it hasn't rained for 400 years?* (questioning/extension)

- *Why don't we see cactuses or other plants in this **desert**?* (questioning/extension)

- *What place have we talked about that would be the opposite of the **desert**?* (questioning)

- *How **windy** is a tornado? A hurricane?* (questioning/extension)

- *How do these **mountains** look different from the other ones we have seen in this book?* (green, no snow) *Why is that? Why aren't there trees on these mountains?* (questioning/extension)

- *What time of year was the illustrator thinking of when he created this picture?* (questioning) *Could that be why there isn't any snow?*

- *Why is a **waterfall** a good name for this?* (questioning)

- *Can you think of any famous **waterfalls** you have heard of?* (examples)

- *Where does the water come from, and where does it go?* (questioning/extension)

- *Does this **toucan** remind you of anything?* (Some students may make the connection to the Froot Loops cereal bird.) (questioning)

- *How is this bird different from the birds we see around our school and homes?* (questioning/extension)

- *We usually think of the water in the ocean as being blue—why did the illustrator make it black?* (questioning)

- *What do you think this is* (pointing to submarine)? (labeling) *Why do divers need* **submarines** *to explore the* **deepest** *parts of the ocean?* (extension)

- *Did you know that some of the fish that live in the* **deep** *ocean have their own lights?* (extension) *How would that help them survive in this environment?* (questioning/extension)

- *The* **iguana** *reminds me of the chameleon/iguanodon* (depending on which stories you have read to your class) *we read about in our other story.* (extension)

- *What happens when a* **volcano erupts**? (questioning/extension)

- *It says that this is the most active* **volcano**. *When you are active, what do you do?* (questioning/definition) *So what do you think it means when we say that a volcano is* **active**? (extension)

- *When it says the most* **extreme**—*what does that mean?* (questioning/definition)

- *I wonder why trees don't grow on top of the* **mountain**. (questioning)

Infusion Activities

Categories: Use the categories suggested by the text— hot, cold, wet, dry, and so on— to generate lists of items. These lists can then be used for a variety of sorting activities.

- Create posters labeled "Wet," "Dry," "Hot," and "Cold." Have students look through magazines for pictures that fit these categories, cut them out, and glue them on the appropriate poster.

Analogies: Some possible analogies are provided below. Remember that these can be done orally or written on the board for independent work if your students' reading level is adequate. Always be sure to have students explain their reasoning. The resulting discussion helps build and solidify word knowledge.

- **Desert** is to **hot** as Antarctica is to _____. (**cold**)

- **Rainforest** is to **wet** as **desert** is to _____. (**dry**)

- **Tree frog** is to **rainforest** as **camel** is to _____. (**desert**)

Line It Up: Details of planning a Line It Up activity are provided in Chapter 3 on pages 25–26. For this example, you might select the words *rainforest, desert, river,*

Using Read-Alouds to Teach Vocabulary © 2011 by Karen J. Kindle, Scholastic Teaching Resources

lake, mountain, and *volcano*. The clues you provide should match information you have given the students during your read-aloud and discussions.

- *In the first spot, put the word that names a place that is very dry. It doesn't get much rain.* (desert)

- *Next, put the word that names a very wet place—a place where it rains a lot.* (rainforest)

- *The next word is a place where water collects, such as a deep pool.* (lake)

- *This word is a body of water too, but the water is moving toward the sea.* (river)

- *The highest place on earth is at the top of one of these.* (mountain)

- *You would not want to be on one of these when it erupted!* (volcano)

Writing: A variety of writing prompts can be developed to provide opportunities for students to use words and concepts from the text in written expression.

- Have students draw a picture of their family and write sentences to respond to questions using comparatives and superlatives such as the following: *Who is the oldest, youngest, tallest, shortest in your family?*

- Students can write about which place on earth they would like to visit. They can describe the things they would see there. This type of project will lead to additional research in books and on the Internet.

Math: This text is perfect for math activities that compare numbers and for measurement. Adjust the lengths to match your students' understanding of numbers. Three examples appear below. Problems can be presented pictorially for our youngest readers.

- *Mountain A is 3,125 feet high. Mountain B is 29,028 feet high. Mountain C is 10,569 feet high. Which mountain is the highest?*

- *River A is 2 miles long. River B is 4 miles long. River C is 5 miles long. Which river is the longest?*

- *Tom is 5 years old. His brother Bobby is 2 years old, and his sister Mary is 7 years old. Which child in the family is the oldest?*

This type of question can be constructed with many of the words from the story: Which place is the snowiest, deepest, windiest, wettest, and so on. You can model the use of comparative language patterns as well. For example, you might draw three mountains on the board and label them A, B, and C. Describe the relationships saying something like this: "Mountain A is high. Mountain C is higher. Mountain B is the highest."

You can also explore geometric shapes after discussing the pyramids depicted in the text. Help your students construct paper pyramids and use these models to discover which shapes are used to make the base and sides of pyramids.

Social Studies: There are obvious and natural connections to your social studies content with this text. Some suggestions are provided below. Items in parentheses are not specifically mentioned in the main text but are referred to in the insets; for example, the word *rainforest* is mentioned in the inset on the page describing the wettest place on earth.

- Landforms: mountain, desert, rainforest, volcano, waterfall

- Bodies of water: river, sea, ocean, lake

- Map skills: locating continents, oceans, and so on

- Continents: Africa, South America, North America, Antarctica

- Countries: United States, Russia, Libya, Colombia, Chile, Venezuela, India, Philippines, Ecuador, Canada, Mexico, Japan, Italy

Students can create maps of an imaginary country or continent with a desert, high mountain, long river, deep ocean, and so on, to demonstrate their understanding of these terms. Creating a map legend will give them an opportunity to use the words in writing and conversation as they describe their continent. Students can practice using comparatives and superlatives as they identify the highest mountain or longest river on their map. You could provide a list of words and illustrations generated from the story and have students create on their own. Students can name the geographic features on their maps—Mount Karen and Long River. You might provide some general guidelines to set minimum expectations such as the following:

1. Show three mountains on your map.

2. Show three rivers on your map.

3. A deep ocean is around your continent.

4. There are two deep lakes on your continent.

Science: The extreme contrasts in environment presented in this text lead nicely into discussions on how animals are suited to their environments. Create trioramas for several of the habitats referred to in the text, such as the desert, polar regions, and rainforest. Students can use additional resources to identify other animals that make these places their homes and add them to the trioramas. Lead them in a discussion about the physical features that help animals survive in harsh conditions.

Cafeteria: While we don't want our students playing with their food, it is possible to bring some of these vocabulary words into the lunchroom.

- *Your mashed potatoes and gravy look like a mountain in the middle of a lake.*

- *That soda can erupted just like a volcano!*

- *The spilt milk is running off the table just like a waterfall.*

Using Read-Alouds to Teach Vocabulary © 2011 by Karen J. Kindle, Scholastic Teaching Resources

UNIT 2

Dig Dig Digging by Margaret Mayo

Text description: *Students are fascinated with construction vehicles and other large trucks. This engaging text will appeal to young children with its rhythmic and repetitive language. The predictable nature of the language makes this a great text for students to read independently when you are finished with your instruction.*

Each page has the name of a vehicle as a title, a colorful illustration of the vehicle in action, and brief text. It concludes with the refrain "they can work all day," making it great for student engagement. The illustrations are simple, but present a lot of things to talk about.

Vocabulary for Instruction

Possible target words: *scoop, lift, tip, huge, engine, race, hose, swoosh, plow, field, squelch, fly, gobble, squeeze, squash, crane, transporter, ramp, vroom, load, rumble, tumble, rescue, helicopter, whir, hover, zoom, rotor, blades, whizz, tar, bulldozer, scrape, shove, tread, grip, long-distance*

Action words: *dig, scoop, lift, tip, race, flash, swoosh, pull, plow, gobble, squeeze, squash, loading, dump, rumble, tumble, rescue, hover, zoom, whizz, press, smooth, spread, flatten, push, scrape, shove, grip, travel, spin*

Sounds: *swoosh, squelch, vroom, crash, whir, beep, sshh*

Vehicles: *back hoe, fire engine, tractor, garbage truck, crane, transporters, dump trucks, helicopter, road roller, bulldozer, trucks*

Miscellaneous: *caterpillar, treads, long-distance, earth, huge, hose, field, bricks, ramps, shiny, rotor blades*

During Reading

During a picture walk, use a combination of *labeling* and *questioning* strategies, since it is likely that your students will have some familiarity with the vehicles depicted in the illustrations. If they seem to have a good grasp on the basics, you should use *extensions* to provide additional information about how these vehicles are used. The illustrations will provide you with lots of ideas; for example, in the first illustration, you can show students how the digger scoops up the earth to make a hole or lifts the dirt into the dump truck to haul away.

This text is also rich in action words that are perfect for *imagery*. Use simple hand motions and gestures to demonstrate words such as *scoop* and *hover* to enhance your students' comprehension. Incorporate sound effects with words such as *beep-beep* or *vroom* to help them understand the concept of onomatopoeia.

Here are some specific suggestions for strategies to use while reading the first few pages of *Dig Dig Digging*.

- Use hand gestures to demonstrate the motions associated with **scooping, lifting,** and **tipping**. (imagery)

- *This digger is making a **huge** hole. It is a really big hole.* (synonym)

- *This digger is also called a **back hoe**. Why is that so?* Help students notice the steering wheel on the right. The worker/operator turns in his seat and uses the levers to make the shovel part work. (extension)

- ***Fire engines**—sometimes we call them fire trucks.* (synonym)

- *Why do fire trucks need to **race**?* (questioning/extension)

- *Look how this fireman is using the **hose** to spray water on the fire* (pointing to hose to label). (labeling)

- *How else do **fire trucks/engines** warn other drivers that they are **racing** down the street?* (extension)

- *The **tractors** have big wheels, just like the diggers. Why do you think these big trucks need such big wheels?* (questioning/extension)

- *It says the dirt is **flying**. The wheels make the dirt go flying. What do you think that means?* (context)

There are a few spots in the text to pay special attention to. First, in a few places the use of metaphor and personification might need additional explanation. For example, the garbage trucks are described as garbage eaters who gobble up trash all day. You might ask if the truck is alive or not, and lead them to notice that the author uses certain words to make us think about how the garbage truck is like a person eating. Show students that the back of the truck looks a little bit like a mouth. The last page of the text continues the metaphor as the author describes the vehicles as resting, asking the reader to be quiet so they can sleep: "Sshh! They can rest all night." You may want to point out how the illustrator makes the fire engines look as though they have faces.

An additional feature to point out during reading is the use of the layout of the text to support meaning. The page discussing trucks provides several great examples of this. The word *long-distance* is stretched way out, and extra space is inserted between the letters

Using Read-Alouds to Teach Vocabulary © 2011 by Karen J. Kindle, Scholastic Teaching Resources

in *long* as well. The letters in the word *tall* are elongated, and the letters in the word *different* go up and down. These features would be wonderful to duplicate in a Picture It infusion activity.

Infusion Activities

Categories: The variety of vehicles presented in this text provides some great opportunities for putting words into categories.

Odd Man Out: Students identify which vehicle does not belong. Be sure to have them explain their thinking—you might be surprised at what they come up with!

- *fire truck, tractor, helicopter, dump truck* (A helicopter flies.)
- *digger, dump truck, bulldozer, crane* (A bulldozer has caterpillar treads.)
- *tractor, fire truck, transporter, garbage truck* (A fire truck is a rescue vehicle.)

Sorting vehicles: Write vehicle names on cards or sentence strips and have students help you sort them by different criteria such as the following:

- Number of wheels
- Vehicles that push, pull, lift, dig, carry, and so on
- Construction vehicles, helping vehicles, transportation vehicles

Analogies: Analogies can be written on the board or completed orally.

- **Crane** is to **lift** as **tractor** is to _____. (**pull**)
- **Roller** is to tar as **bulldozer** is to _____. (**earth**)
- **Transporter** is to cars as **garbage truck** is to _____. (trash)

Act It Out: The action words in this book are easy to act out. Write words such as *lift, tip, spin, scoop, pull, race, roll,* and *shove* on cards. Students can draw a card and act out the motion for the others to guess.

Picture It: As I mentioned earlier, the text uses varied fonts and spacing to depict word meaning. A few examples are provided below, but you and your students will be able to come up with ideas for many more of the words in the book.

L   O   N   G   TALL   r a m p

Phonological and phonemic awareness: This text seems most appropriate to me for our younger students, so phonological and phonemic awareness activities are important to include. A wide variety of skills can be reviewed using the target words, including the following:

- *Counting syllables:* Have students clap the syllable in the following words: *truck, trans/por/ter, hel/i/cop/ter, bull/do/zer, dig/ger, trac/tor.*

- *Identifying initial and final phonemes:*
  - *What sound do you hear at the beginning of* truck, tractor, *and* transporter?
  - *What sound to you hear at the end of* swoosh, push, *and* squash?

- *Beginning sound bingo:* As you give clues for the following words, be sure to provide definitions or sentences that present the word in context: *bulldozer, cranes, dig, engine, fire, gobble, holes, lift, pull, race, scoop, tractor, vroom, work.*

Writing: There are many possibilities for writing activities based on this text. Here are just a few.

- *Labeling:* Provide students with small sticky notes and let them create labels for items that they see in the illustrations; for example, they might make labels for "wheels," "rocks," "cones," and so on.

- Create a list of the sound words from the text. Brainstorm additional words to add. Students can select several words and create a little book about sounds, perhaps by using a sentence frame such as *The car goes vroom* or *The doorbell goes ring-ring.*

Music: Adapt the vehicles and words from the text to "The Wheels on the Bus." Students can help create new verses with other vehicles not mentioned in the book. Support word learning by adding appropriate movements and sounds.

> The diggers work hard; they dig and dig,
> Scoop and scoop, lift and lift.
> They make huge holes as they dig, dig, dig.
> They can work all day.
>
> The tractors work hard, they pull and pull,
> Pull and pull, pull and pull.
> Plowing up the fields with a squelch, squelch, squelch.
> They can work all day.
>
> The cranes work hard, they lift and lift,
> Lift and lift, lift and lift.
> Up go the bricks to the top of the building,
> They can work all day.

Using Read-Alouds to Teach Vocabulary © 2011 by Karen J. Kindle, Scholastic Teaching Resources

UNIT 3

Biggest, Strongest, Fastest by Steve Jenkins

Text description: *If you have glanced through this chapter, you may have noticed that Steve Jenkins's name shows up a lot. Jenkins is one of my new favorites. His distinctive artwork is appealing, and there is always a lot to talk about in his books. Although this particular text is not really new, it was new to me and may be to you as well. As the title implies, this is a book of superlatives. Students are introduced to the concepts such as biggest, strongest, and fastest with both familiar and unfamiliar animals, and with some unexpected twists. As we saw with* Hottest, Coldest, Highest, Deepest, *there are two levels of text to explore—the text itself and the insets. Don't overlook the chart on the last page of the book. You will find it very helpful in answering the many questions your students will have about what these animals eat and where they live.*

Vocabulary for Instruction

Possible target words: *blue whale, African elephant, giraffe, shrew, mammal, hummingbird, acrobatic, jellyfish, animal, tentacles, poisonous, filaments, stun, antelope, electric, eel, shock, volts, anaconda, prey, flea, tortoise*

Animals: *blue whale, African elephant, ant, giraffe, Etruscan shrew, bee hummingbird, sun jellyfish, bird spider, cheetah, electric eel, land snail, anaconda, flea, tortoise*

Miscellaneous: *crawl, microscope, mammal, teaspoon, shock, acrobatic, tentacles, poisonous, filaments, stun, electric, shock, volts, prey*

During Reading

The strategies you are most likely to use while reading this text are *clarification* and *extension*. Most of your students will know at least a little bit about the majority of animals in this text, so simple definitions will not be needed in most cases. You may find, however, that the information they do know is limited, and so extensions are required to give additional information. For example, your students will probably recognize the elephant from seeing its picture in books or at the zoo, but they may know little about how the animal actually lives in the wild. They may also have false information that needs clarification or correction. Young children often think that a whale is a fish and need clarification to understand that it is a mammal.

The following statements are suggestions of questions and comments you might make while reading the text to promote word learning:

- *What does this mean: "They are the record holders of the animal world"?* (extension)

- *So this is the **elephant**. Can you show me his trunk and tusks?* (reverse labeling)

- *The **elephant's** big ears help keep it cool. It flaps them like giant fans.* (extension)

- *This little picture down here shows how big an adult human would be if he were standing next to an **elephant**. He is about the size of one leg!* (extension)

- *The strongest animal for its size is the _____.* (Read the page without showing the picture. Have students predict which animal name should go in the blank.) *The **ant**? How can a little ant be the strongest animal? Oh wait, I see now. It says "for its size." An ant can carry five ants. To be as strong as an ant, the **elephant** would have to be able to carry five elephants!* (extension)

- *How many legs does the **ant** have? Now I know an ant is an insect, because insects have six legs.* (extension)

- *With that big, long neck, what do you think the **giraffe** eats?* (questioning/extension)

- ***Whales** live in the sea, but they are not fish. What happens to a fish if you take it out of the water? But a whale needs to come up to the surface to breathe.* (clarification)

- *The smallest bird is the **bee hummingbird**. It weighs less than a dime. Put a dime on your hand—you can hardly even feel that something is there!* (extension)

- *What do you think this bird eats? Does its long beak give you a clue?* (questioning/extension)

- ***Hummingbirds** are different from other birds because they can **hover** like helicopters. They can stay in one place as they fly.* (definition/extension)

- *Is a **spider** an insect? Let's count how many legs it has. Remember we said that insects have six legs. The spider has eight legs, so it isn't an insect.* (clarification)

- *Why do you think this spider is called a **bird spider**? Its web is strong enough to catch birds!* (questioning/extension)

- *How is the **anaconda's** tongue different from other animals' tongues?* (questioning/extension)

Using Read-Alouds to Teach Vocabulary © 2011 by Karen J. Kindle, Scholastic Teaching Resources

- *How do you think this snake catches its prey?* **Prey** *means the animals that the snake catches for food.* (definition and extension)
- *This* **tortoise** *looks like a big turtle. I wonder how tortoises and turtles are different.* (questioning)

Infusion Activities

Categories: Discuss classifications of animals—mammal, reptile, fish, bird, amphibian. Take the animals presented in the text and sort them into the appropriate groups. Brainstorm additional animals for each group or "collect" them from other nonfiction texts.

Analogies: Analogies help students see relationships between words and concepts. Always be sure to have students explain their answers and encourage multiple ways of responding.

- **Flea** is to insect as **whale** is to _____. (**mammal**)
- **Cheetah** is to run as **snail** is to _____. (**crawl**)
- **Elephant** is to large as **shrew** is to _____. (small)

Line It Up: Select the names of five or six animals and have students write those words on cards. You can also do this activity as a whole group with one set of cards and a pocket chart. You can play the game several times, giving different clues about the animals based on the information from the book and what you have provided with your extensions. For the elephant, for example, you might use the following clues on different days.

- *This animal is the largest land animal.*
- *This animal has a trunk and tusks. The trunk is like a long nose and the tusks are special long teeth.*
- *This animal has large ears that it flaps to help keep itself cool in the hot African sun.*

Be sure your clues reinforce word meanings and information. You can repeat the game with different animals.

Clothesline: The animals in this book work well with a clothesline activity. Write the animal names on cards and have students put them in order. You might have students place them from fastest to slowest or from smallest to largest. You can also put this activity in a center and have students refer to the last page of the book so they gain practice in gathering information from charts and in comparing numbers. For example, you might write *ant, blue whale, shrew, jellyfish, bird spider, cheetah, eel, anaconda,* and *tortoise* on cards. Using the chart, students can place these animals in order from shortest to longest.

Writing: Have your students draw pictures of and write about their favorite animals. You can combine their individual pages into a class book about animals. Some students will enjoy learning about other animals and creating a chart that shows the information they have found.

Math: During one of your readings of the text, have a ruler handy to show students the lengths mentioned in the text. For example, while reading the page on the shrew, you might say something like this:

- *This says that the length from the tip of its tail to the tip of its nose is only 2½ inches. Let's use our inch rulers to see what that looks like. It's a little longer than my thumb, but not as long as my index (pointer) finger.*

Other ways in which you might incorporate measurement concepts into your reading are described below:

- *Keep your inch rulers handy. This little hummingbird is only 3 inches long. So is it bigger or smaller than the shrew?*

- *The snail is very slow! It can only move 8 inches in a minute. Let's time that. Let's mark off 8 inches—now your finger is a snail. Can you move that slowly? I'll tell you when to stop moving.*

- *The flea is very small, but it is the world's best jumper. Even though it looks kind of big in this picture, the flea is really, really tiny. It is only 1/16 of an inch—that is smaller than one little mark on this inch ruler! What could the flea be the best at doing? It can jump 8 inches. That doesn't seem very far, but it is for something the size of the flea. Remember how we talked about the ant being strong because it can carry 5 times its weight? Well, the flea can jump 130 times its own height! If you could do that, you would be able to jump to the top of the school building without even trying! You'd be able to jump even much higher than that!*

If you are working on measurement in math, you might want to help your students begin to conceptualize some of the big numbers in this text. For example, you could take your class out to the playground and show them the actual length of the jellyfish.

- *The sun jellyfish has tentacles that are 200 feet long. How far is that? Let's see. If we had a sun jellyfish here and could stretch out a tentacle, how far on the playground would it go?* (Take predictions.) *Okay let's find out. I have a piece of yarn here that is 200 feet long. Let's stretch it out and see!*

Science: The illustrations in this book work well for creating diagrams. Show your students how to create labels for different body parts using sticky notes. They can then

Using Read-Alouds to Teach Vocabulary © 2011 by Karen J. Kindle, Scholastic Teaching Resources

draw their own animals and label key items. You can find simple drawings of animals on the Internet as well.

Recess: Competitive activities must be handled carefully, but your students might enjoy seeing who in their class is like the cheetah (fastest runner) and who is like the flea (farthest jumper). You can also work the following ideas into your conversations with students:

- *My goodness, you ran so fast I thought you were a cheetah!*

- *You are all jumping so high that you are jumping just like fleas!*

UNIT 4

What Do You Do With a Tail Like This?
by Steve Jenkins & Robin Page

Text description: *This text works really well if you are working on a science unit related to animals or the five senses. It describes how animals use their noses, ears, tails, eyes, mouths, and feet in ways that are unique. Jenkins' captivating artwork draws readers in by showing only part of the animals, leading students to predict what the animals will be and how they use different parts of their bodies.*

Unless you are an animal expert yourself, you will want to read the information about the animals provided in the back of the book. They are presented by body part, in the order in which they appear in the text. Your students are sure to have questions about all of these amazing animals, and the interesting facts presented here are sure to amaze them. This section is a valuable resource for the extensions that you include in your instruction.

Vocabulary for Instruction

Possible target words: *platypus, hyena, elephant, mole, alligator, jackrabbit, bat, hippopotamus, cricket, humpback whale, brush, pesky, giraffe, skunk, lizard, scorpion, nasty, sting, eagle, chameleon, horned lizard, squirt, chimpanzee, water strider, mountain goat, leap, ledge, gecko, pelican, scoop, mosquito, anteater, termites, capture, archer, archerfish, stream*

Animals: The text uses simplified names for some of the animals, but the authors provide the complete names at the end of the book; the full names are included in parentheses: *platypus, hyena, elephant (African elephant), mole (star-nosed mole), alligator (American alligator), jackrabbit (antelope jackrabbit), bat (yellow-wing bat), cricket (field cricket), hippopotamus, humpback whale, giraffe, skunk (striped), lizard (skink), scorpion, monkey (spider monkey), eagle (bald eagle), chameleon, four-eyed fish, bush baby, horned lizard, chimpanzee, blue-footed booby, water strider, gecko, mountain goat, pelican, anteater, termites, mosquito, archerfish, egg-eating snake*

Body parts: *nose, ears, tails, eyes, mouths, feet, tongue*

Miscellaneous: *brush, pesky, squirt, ledge, scoop, capture, sting, leap, scoop, archer, stream*

When you work with this text, you'll find a lot of opportunities to add more vocabulary words. For example, when looking at the page on noses, you might show students how we all have *nostrils*, how the hyena has *whiskers*, or how the platypus' nose is like a duck's *bill*.

During Reading

A wide variety of strategies is needed when reading this text. Some of the animals will be unfamiliar to students, so labeling and definitions are the most appropriate. In other cases, the students may be able to identify the animal but have incomplete information or some misunderstandings; for example, they might identify the antelope jackrabbit as a bunny. You will need to provide clarification.

Use extensions widely as you provide additional information about these animals and the ways that the special body parts help them find food, protect them against predators, or help them survive in their specific environments.

Suggestions for incorporating these strategies into your read-aloud include the following:

- *The **platypus** uses his **nose** like a shovel to dig in the mud for food.* (extension)

- *We predicted that this **nose** belonged to a dog. It looks a little like a dog's nose, doesn't it? How is this nose different from a dog's nose?* (clarification)

- *Did you know that **elephants** could do this with their **noses**? Their **noses** are called trunks.* (definition, extension)

- *This **mole** is called a **star-nosed mole**.* (labeling) *Is that a good name for this animal?* (questioning) *These little fingers help the **mole** travel in the dark underground tunnels and find food.* (extension and/or clarification)

Using Read-Alouds to Teach Vocabulary © 2011 by Karen J. Kindle, Scholastic Teaching Resources

- *This part looks like an insect's leg. How could it be an **ear**?* (clarification)
- *How do you think the **jackrabbit's** big **ears** help it stay cool?* (questioning/extension)
- *The authors say that the **bat** can see with its **ears**. How can you see with your ears?* (clarification)
- *The **cricket's ears** are on its knees. Ears on your knees? Imagine how that would work for you!* (extension)
- *If you were a **hippopotamus**, you could close your **ears** when you were taking a bath or swimming. Then you wouldn't get water in them.* (extension)
- Before showing the picture of the **tails**, have students predict which animals might have special tails. They may think of animals such as the **skunk**. It is a good chance to see what they already know. (extension)
- *The **giraffe** has his own built-in fly swatter. What do we use if a **pesky** fly keeps bothering us? Right, we swat it with our hands. But the giraffe can't do that—so he uses his **tail**. The long hair on the tip makes it much easier to brush away more flies. Pretend there is a pesky fly bothering you right now. Take your hand and brush it away, just like the giraffe would do with his tail.* (synonym, extension, imagery)
- *This **skunk** is doing a handstand. Do you know why? When an enemy is in front of the skunk, he doesn't want to turn his back, so he does a handstand. This way, the skunk can spray his enemy but also see it at all times.* (extension)
- *This type of **lizard** is called a **skink**. If another animal grabs its **tail**, the skink can break off the tail and get away. Then the skink grows a new tail!* (extension)
- *At the end of the scorpion's tail, you can see a **stinger**.* (labeling) *The **scorpion** uses its **tail** to catch its prey. The stinger has poison on it that paralyzes the animal. That means the animal can't move to get away.* (extension and definition)
- *The **chameleon** can look two ways at once. We can't do that. Our eyes work mostly together. But a chameleon could see Jonathan way over there, and Monique way over here at the same time. I think I would like to be able to do that!* (extension)
- *The **four-eyed fish** doesn't really have four **eyes**, but his eyeballs are divided so that he has two places to see out of. So when the four-eyed fish is at the top of the water like this* (pointing to picture), *one part of the eye can see above the water and one part can see below. Why do you think this helps the fish?* (extension)

- *Mountains aren't smooth and flat; they have lots of **ledges**—kind of like shelves of rock.* (definition) ***Mountain goats** can **leap**, or jump, from ledge to ledge without slipping and falling.* (synonym, extension)

- *The **pelican** has a special beak. The lower part of its beak is softer and can be used like a net to **scoop** up fish* (making scooping motion)—*the way we use a net in a fish tank to scoop up the fish when we change the water.* (extension, imagery)

- *Even though these animals are called **anteaters**, they actually eat insects called **termites**.* (clarification) *Look at this picture of a termite mound.* (labeling) *How does having a long snout and **tongue** help the anteater get its food? What do you think it uses these long claws for?* (labeling, questioning/extension)

- *An archer is someone who uses a bow and arrow.* (definition) *Is **archerfish** a good name for this fish?* (questioning/extension)

Infusion Activities

Categories: The organization of *What Do You Do With a Tail Like This?* contains some natural groupings for sorts. For instance, you can write the animal names on cards and then place them into categories by nose, ears, tails, eyes, feet, mouth—remembering of course to tell your students that these are special features but that many of the animals have all these characteristics. You might also sort the animals by mammal, fish, bird, or reptile.

Some possible *Odd Man Out* examples include the following:

- *pelican, eagle, bat, blue-footed booby* (A bat is a mammal.)

- *cricket, mosquito, lizard, water strider* (A lizard is not an insect.)

- *mountain goat, alligator, platypus, hippopotamus* (A mountain goat does not live in water.)

Analogies: You can make the analogies easy or difficult, depending on the level of knowledge and development of your students.

- Fish is to **pelican** as **termite** is to _____. (**anteater**)

- Feathers are to birds as scales are to _____. (**lizards**)

Line It Up: As you saw with some of the previous books on animals, the animals you choose and the clues you create will depend on the things you have highlighted in your discussions. Even though the animals' names might seem the obvious choice for this

Using Read-Alouds to Teach Vocabulary © 2011 by Karen J. Kindle, Scholastic Teaching Resources

game, don't forget that there are plenty of other words to target for instruction such as *brush, pesky, squirt, ledge, scoop,* and *capture.*

- *This word is a synonym for annoying.* (pesky) *Put this word in the first position.*

- *The second word is something you might do to get rid of a fly that was bothering you. It also can mean something you do to your hair.* (brush)

- *You might do this to get some catsup on your fries. The horned lizard does this to scare off enemies.* (squirt) *This word goes in the third place.*

- *The fourth word is like a shelf in the rocks. A mountain goat can jump or leap on these to climb.* (ledge)

- *A pelican does this to catch fish from the ocean. You might also use this to get ice cream onto a cone.* (scoop) *Put this word in the fifth position.*

- *A synonym for this word might be* catch. (capture) *This is the last word.*

Act It Out: Some of the distinctive movements described in this text are good for acting out. You can write an animal's name on a card and then have students think about how they would act it out; for example, a child might act out an eagle by flapping his arms as though he were flying, then holding his hand above his eyes as though he was looking far away to show that the eagle has great eyesight. Other students guess which animal the child is pretending to be. You can make this a little easier by giving your students a set of choices. Be sure to have students explain their answers as shown below.

- *You're right, Carla. What were the clues Mary gave that made you think of an eagle?*

You can also provide additional extensions.

- *Good job, Mary. You remembered that eagles can see far away. They can see four to eight times better than people.*

A variation of this activity would be to give the child a phrase to act out such as a *pelican scooping fish from the water* or *a mountain goat leaping from ledge to ledge.* Be sure to include as many target words as possible.

Phonological and phonemic awareness: Students enjoy learning about compound words, and there are several in this text to work with, including *jackrabbit, humpback, archerfish,* and *anteater.* If you routinely work on phonological awareness activities with deletion, you can easily substitute these words.

- *Say* jackrabbit. *Now say it without the* jack.
- *Say* humpback. *Now say it without the* hump.

If your students are more advanced in their deletion skills, you can try some more difficult examples.

- *Say* goat. *Now say it without the* /g/.

- *Say* skink. *Now say it without the* /s/.

As always, use this opportunity to reinforce word meaning.

Writing: Talk with your students about how the animals' names describe something about their appearance: The yellow-winged bat has yellow wings; the star-nosed mole has a nose that looks like a star; and the horned lizard has little horns or spikes on it. Inspire students' creativity by asking, "I wonder what a blue-winged bat would look like? Or a six-eyed fish instead of a four-eyed fish?" Students can create their own original animals, name them, and write about where they live, what they eat, and how they catch their food.

Math: It's very easy to incorporate these animal names and other words into your math word problems for the day.

- *There were 6 pesky flies on the giraffe's back. He brushed away 4 flies with his tail. How many flies were left?*

- *A water strider has 6 legs. How many legs would 2 water striders have?*

Science: As with the other animal books discussed in this chapter, you can easily find links to your curricular objectives. Whether you are focusing on the senses, classifications, or habitats, you can find a way to incorporate your target words into your science units.

Recess: While you are outside with your students, look for opportunities to point out animals they may see and talk about their characteristics.

- *Look at that hawk circling up in the sky. I wonder if he can see as well as an eagle? Do you think the hawk is looking for food?*

- *There's a cricket. Remember, he can use the ears on his knees to hear you coming.*

- *It's hot out today. If we had big ears like the jackrabbit, do you think we would stay cool?*

 Using Read-Alouds to Teach Vocabulary © 2011 by Karen J. Kindle, Scholastic Teaching Resources

UNIT 5

It's Pumpkin Time! by Zoe Hall

Text description: *In this fun story, two children plant their pumpkin patch to get ready for their favorite holiday—Halloween. The simple text, large type, and colorful illustrations are perfect for reading aloud. The back page shows how the pumpkin seeds grow underground, so students are able to see the roots and how the shoots come up. This is a great companion text for* Pumpkin, Pumpkin *(Titherington 1986) described in Chapter 6 on page 103. It reinforces many of the same concepts, but each book has a unique presentation that students will enjoy.*

Vocabulary for Instruction

> **Possible target words:** *holiday, jack-o'-lantern, patch, soil, shovel, spade, narrow, seeds, tiny, roots, shoots, poke, vines, weeds, buds, flowers, bloom, wheelbarrow, hollow, costumes*
>
> **Multiple meaning words:** *plant, patch, turn, rows, cover, shoots*
>
> **New terms for familiar concepts:** *jack-o'-lantern, soil, narrow, poke, tiny, costumes*
>
> **New terms:** *shovel, spade, bloom, wheelbarrow, hollow*
>
> **Content terms:** *seeds, roots, shoots, vines, buds, flowers, pumpkins, stem, leaf*

During Reading

Most of your students will be very familiar with the traditional activities associated with Halloween, such as carving pumpkins, donning costumes, and going trick-or-treating. Your ELL students, particularly if they are newcomers, will need your help in understanding these customs so they can share in the fun. You will also need to be sensitive to students who do not celebrate Halloween. You can still use this great text, but stop when the children take the pumpkins home.

As with all of the texts, you can use a variety of strategies with this book. If your students are unfamiliar with most of the words, you will want to use more labeling. If your students are already fairly familiar with these words and concepts, you can include more extensions. Here are some suggestions for your readings:

- *Holidays are special days. Can you think of some holidays that you celebrate?* (examples)

- *Soil is another word for dirt.* (synonym)

- *This is a shovel.* (labeling)

- *It says they turn the soil with a shovel. Look at the picture and tell me what you think it means to turn the soil?* (questioning, context)

- *How is a shovel different from a spade?* (Have real tools or pictures to share.) *A spade has a flat blade, so it is good to use to make the rows for planting the seeds.* (extension)

- *The roots are the part of the plant that grows under the ground. They take in the nutrients, or food, and water from the ground for the plant to grow.* (definition, extension)

- *The shoots are the little parts we can see here—kind of like baby plants.* (labeling)

- *Look how the shoots have grown into vines.* (labeling) *You can see how the newer parts of the vines are thinner and the leaves are smaller.* (extension)

- *What is the boy using to water the plants?* (questioning)

- *These little round parts are the buds. As they get a little bigger, they will open up into these yellow flowers.* (labeling, extension)

- *I didn't know that, did you? I thought pumpkins were always orange. I guess pumpkins are like bananas and other fruit. Sometimes you get them from the store, and they aren't totally ripe yet, so they still have green on them.* (extension)

- *The pumpkins grow all summer, and in the fall they start to change color. Can you see all the colors in them? First they were green and now they are yellow—and they are just starting to turn to orange.* (extension)

- *A wheelbarrow is a small cart with two wheels.* (definition) *Here is a picture of one.* (labeling) *Do any of you have a wheelbarrow in your garage or shed? Mom and Dad might use it for their yard work.*

Infusion Activities

Categories: These examples are fairly simple, but since this text is most likely to appeal to younger students, I think that is appropriate. You can always make them more difficult if your students are able to handle the challenge.

Using Read-Alouds to Teach Vocabulary © 2011 by Karen J. Kindle, Scholastic Teaching Resources

Odd Man Out: Students identify which word doesn't belong and explain why.

- *shovel, spade, wheelbarrow, patch* (A patch is not a tool.)
- *seed, root, shoot, hollow* (*Hollow* is an adjective.)

To build vocabulary, you can also help students brainstorm items that belong in various categories. When brainstorming, they are generating examples of the category, which is one of the vocabulary strategies used to develop word knowledge.

- *Shovels, spades, and wheelbarrows are all tools that you might use in the garden. What are some other tools you might need?* (Watering can [pictured on title page and on page with the water]; students might mention hoe, hose, trowel, and so on.)

Analogies: Analogies such as these help students see relationships and make comparisons.

- **Spade** is to dirt as hose is to _____. (water)
- Branch is to trunk as **leaf** is to _____. (**stem**)

Line It Up: Start by having students make word cards with the names of the parts of a plant: *root, seed, stem, leaf, flower, bud*. Provide definitions for your clues. On another day, you might focus on the phonemic aspects of the words by providing different clues.

- *The first word has the short /e/ sound.* (stem)
- *The next word has the short /u/ sound.* (bud)
- *The third word has the long /e/ sound spelled with a double letter.* (seed)
- *The fourth word is a two-syllable word that has the /ow/ sound in the first part.* (flower)
- *The fifth word also has the long /e/ sound, but this one has two different letters in the middle.* (leaf)
- *The last word has the /oo/ sound like boot.* (root)

Clothesline: Prepare word cards with the following words from the story: *seed, roots, vine, bud, flower, pumpkin*. Students can put the words in order based on the growth sequence of a pumpkin plant.

Act It Out: Students can act out many parts of the story. For example, they might act out *turning the soil, planting the seeds, watering the plants, pulling weeds,* or *picking pumpkins.*

Picture It: For the plant parts, try using the word to show the part; for example, for *roots*, you could draw roots under the ground, but the roots would be made up of the letters. I would also suggest writing the word at the top of the card, so students can easily see it in its correct print form.

Phonological and phonemic awareness: Many of you have your students generate lists of words that fit particular phonics patterns. When appropriate, you can use target words for your examples—with an extra emphasis on meaning infused into the lesson.

- *Boys and girls, this word is* root. *That is the part of the plant below the ground that gets nourishment and water to feed the plant. There are some other words in this story that have the same sound* (root, shoot, bloom). *What other words have that sound, too?*

Writing: There are many published thematic units dealing with pumpkins and plants. Most of these will have writing ideas that you can use. When possible, be sure to model infusing your target vocabulary, for example:

- *In your story, you said that you planted your seeds in the dirt. What was that other word for dirt than we learned?* (soil)

Math: The story begins with a question: What is your favorite holiday? This discussion can easily lead into the construction of a graph to show the students' favorite holidays. Word problems such as the following can be added into your daily math lessons.

- *Draw a picture and write a number sentence to solve this problem. In the pumpkin patch, there are 2 vines. Each vine has 3 pumpkins. How many pumpkins are in the pumpkin patch?*

- *Bobby planted 3 rows of seeds in his pumpkin patch. He put 3 seeds in each row. How many pumpkin seeds did he plant?*

- *Bobby has 12 pumpkin seeds. If he plants 3 seeds in each row, how many rows of pumpkins will he have in the patch?* (You can have students glue pumpkin seeds to a square of brown paper to illustrate their answers.)

Music: This text is easy to put to music. Think of a familiar tune for your students, and write the lyrics to match the rhythm and rhyme. Songs with repetitive phrases such as the one on page 69 cut down on the work. You can think of a few verses and then let your students help you generate more possibilities. When possible, think of gestures to go with the words to help students remember what they mean. This also increases students' engagement and enjoyment of the activity.

Songs can also be written on charts and used for shared reading activities. You may want to consider teaching students a few verses, and then adding one more each day, leading up to Halloween.

Using Read-Alouds to Teach Vocabulary © 2011 by Karen J. Kindle, Scholastic Teaching Resources

It's Almost Pumpkin Time

(*sing to the tune of "Skip to my Lou"*)

Dig a little hole to plant some seeds,
Dig a little hole to plant some seeds,
Shovels and spades to plant some seeds,
Getting reading for pumpkin time!

Tiny little shoots poke out of the ground,
Tiny little shoots poke out of the ground,
Sunshine and water help them grow,
Getting closer to pumpkin time!

Pumpkin vines growing, inch by inch,
Pumpkin vines growing, inch by inch,
Growing longer every day,
Getting closer to pumpkin time!

Watering the plants and pulling up weeds,
Watering the plants and pulling up weeds,
Giving our plants all the things they need,
Getting closer to pumpkin time!

Yellow flowers show where the pumpkins will grow,
Yellow flowers show where the pumpkins will grow,
Buds turn into flowers, what do you know?
Getting close to pumpkin time!

Little bitty pumpkins, green and small,
Little bitty pumpkins, green and small,
Bigger and bigger, day by day,
It's almost pumpkin time!

Changing color, green to yellow,
Changing color, green to yellow,
Then yellow to orange in the fall,
It's almost pumpkin time!

Time to pick the pumpkins and take them home,
Time to pick the pumpkins and take them home,
Put them in the wheelbarrow and take
them home,
It's almost pumpkin time!

Hollow it out and carve a face,
Hollow it out and carve a face,
A big jack o' lantern glowing bright,
It's finally pumpkin time!

Put on your costumes. Trick or treat.
Put on your costumes. Trick or treat.
Lots of goodies for me to eat,
I love pumpkin time!

Science: The Build a Plant activity described in Chapter 3 on page 33 is a good match for this text if you are focusing on science content dealing with the parts of a plant. You also may want to consider the following suggestions:

- *Matching game:* Create a matching or concentration game in which children must pair picture vocabulary cards with their definitions.

- *Planting seeds:* Students always enjoy planting seeds either in dirt or in clear plastic bags so they can watch them grow. Use the diagrams on the back page of the text to create a chart. Students can use this chart to describe what is happening to their seed in a science/plant journal.

UNIT 6

Dinosaurs by Gail Gibbons

Text description: *Students, especially boys, seem to be fascinated by dinosaurs. They often bring a lot of background knowledge from trips to museums, books, and media sources. Many children have seen animated and film versions of dinosaurs, such as the Jurassic Park movies. Gibbons's text provides factual information in a way that is accessible to young learners. This is a good companion text to* Saturday Night at the Dinosaur Stomp *(Shields, 1997), included in Chapter 6 on pages 107–111. It uses many of the same dinosaur names in a fanciful narrative. You will want to practice saying the dinosaur names in advance!*

Be sure you don't overlook the information included on dinosaur footprints on the last page of the book. This section explains the kind of information that paleontologists can glean from fossilized footprints and will be very important in one of the infusion activities.

Vocabulary for Instruction

Possible target words: Dinosaur names appear under "Dinosaur names": *roam, huge, fossils, footprint, paleontologists, chipped, skeletons, creatures, terrible, remains, peaceful, spikes, plates, protection, enemy, shields, swamp, enormous, fins, oars, beak, swift, terrified, theory, meteor, recent.* Although the terms *carnivore* and *herbivore* are not used in the text, you may want to introduce these terms in your discussions.

Dinosaur names: *ankylosaurus, stegosaurus, protoceratops, triceratops, iguanodon, anatosaurus, apatosaurus, brachiosaurus, pteranodon, elasmosaurus, allosaurus, tyrannosaurus rex*

Science words: *fossils, paleontologists, fins, theory, meteor*

Multiple-meaning words: *plates, spikes, running, remains*

Miscellaneous: *remains, plates, spikes, shields, swamp, huge, enormous, beak, toothless, oars, roamed, terrified, recent, enemies, swift, peaceful, protection, skeletons, creatures, terrible*

During Reading

The specific strategies you choose to utilize during your read-aloud of this text will depend a great deal on your instructional goals, the interests of your students, and of course their prior knowledge. If your students already know a lot about dinosaurs, you will want to focus mainly on *extensions, questioning,* and *context.* If your students know very little, you will want to use *definitions* and *labeling.* The suggestions below make the assumption that you are using this text in response to students' interest, and that they do not possess a great deal of knowledge about dinosaurs.

- *The author says here that some dinosaurs were small.* (point to the small dinosaur) *I always think of dinosaurs as being **enormous**.* (extension)

- ***Huge**—so that is bigger than big, isn't it?* (context)

- *The author says here that a **fossil** is the **remains** of a plant or animal in the rock.* (definition) *So dinosaur bones would be fossils.* (example)

- *See how the **paleontologists** are using these little brooms to sweep the dirt away from the bones? They used this axe* (labeling) *and smaller chisels* (labeling) *to chip away the rock. That means the paleontologists took the rock away in little bits.* (definition)

- *So this* (point to picture) *is a dinosaur's **skeleton**—its bones.* (labeling, synonym)

- ***Ankylosaurus** had **spikes** and **plates*** (labeling) *on its body for **protection**. So the meat-eaters couldn't bite an ankylosaurus very easily.*

- *Look at the **spikes** and **plates*** (point to each) *on the **stegosaurus**. What do you think they were for?* (labeling, questioning)

- *These animals had big **shields** to protect their necks.* (extension) *A shield is something that protects you.* (definition) *Your car has a windshield to protect* *you from the wind and things that might fly up into the car when you drive.* (example)

- ***Iguanodon***. *Does that name remind you of anything?* (questioning) *I have heard of iguanas—I wonder if that is how this dinosaur got its name?*

- *The book says that the* **anatosaurus** *ate water plants from the* **swamp**. *So what do you think a swamp is?* (questioning) *Which clues helped you figure that out?* (context)

- *These two dinosaurs look a lot alike. They both have long necks* (point to illustration) *for getting plants from the water and long tails* (point to illustration) *to help them keep their balance.* (labeling, extension) *Can you think of other animals that have long tails for balance?* (example)

- *This dinosaur looks really different. What does it remind you of? I think so, too. I think it looks a little like a bird or a bat.* (extension)

- *So far, all of the dinosaurs we have talked about are* **herbivores**—*plant eaters. This dinosaur is a* **carnivore**—*that means "meat-eater."* (definition) *Does it remind you of another animal we have read about?* (questioning)

- *This dinosaur used its* **fins** (labeling) *like* **oars** *to paddle through the water— just the way you would use an oar to paddle a boat or canoe.* (extension)

These suggestions do not take you through the entire book, but they should give you a good starting point to complete the reading in ways that meet the needs of your students and match your instructional goals.

Infusion Activities

Categories: There are many different sorting activities that you can do with this text. A few are suggested below:

- Sort by carnivore/herbivore

- Sort by size

- Sort by method of protection (spikes, shields, plates)

- Sort by number of legs, or whether the dinosaur lived in the water or on land

Analogies: The categories you create can provide ideas for analogies, as seen in the following examples.

- **T. rex** is to **carnivore** (or meat) as **apatosaurus** is to _____. (**herbivore**)

- **Triceratops** is to horns as **stegosaurus** is to _____. (**plates** or **spikes**)

Using Read-Alouds to Teach Vocabulary © 2011 by Karen J. Kindle, Scholastic Teaching Resources

Line It Up: Even though the dinosaur names are too difficult for most if not all of your students to read—and I wouldn't have them try to copy the words on their own cards—you can do this Line It Up activity as a group with the pocket chart. Begin with *triceratops, stegosaurus, pteranodon, T. rex,* and *iguanodon.* You can repeat the activity on subsequent days with other dinosaur names.

- *This dinosaur had three horns. Here is a hint: A tricycle has three wheels. Put this card in the first spot at the bottom right side of your desk.* (triceratops)

- *This dinosaur had four long spikes on the end of its tail to protect itself. Put this card to the right of the first.* (stegosaurus)

- *This dinosaur could fly like a bird. This card is in the third spot.* (pteranodon)

- *This dinosaur had teeth that were six inches long. Put this card in the fourth spot.* (T. rex)

- *This dinosaur's name sounds like a lizard we learned about. It has spiked thumbs for protection. This is the last card.* (iguanadon)

You can also use simpler words to create the usual Line It Up activity where all the students have their own sets of word cards. Use target words that will have higher utility such as *plate, spike, shield, footprint,* and *fossil.*

- *This word means something that some dinosaurs like stegosauruses had on their backs for protection. It is also something you might eat off of.* (plate)

- *Stegosaurus had four of these long sharp things on its tail.* (spike)

- *Some dinosaurs had these on their necks so other dinosaurs couldn't bite them.* (shield)

- *Paleontologists learn about dinosaurs by studying these.* (This clue will work for two word cards: fossils and skeletons.)

Clothesline: This text uses several words to indicate size, making it a good text for a clothesline activity. The words in the text are *small, big, huge,* and *enormous.* You could add other words for size such as *tiny, little, large,* or *massive.* As your students put the dinosaurs in order on the clothesline, remember that there are no exact answers for this activity.

Phonological and phonemic awareness: Repeat the Line It Up activity shown above using clues about the phonological properties of the target words. Because you want your students to focus on this aspect, keep your clues short and simple such as the following:

- *This first word is a compound word.* (footprint)

- *The second word is a two-syllable word, but it is not a compound word.* (fossil)

- *The third word has the long /e/ sound.* (shield)

- *The next word has a long /i/ sound.* (spike)

- *The final word rhymes with* gate. (plate)

As you check students' work, you can infuse additional review of word meanings, as seen in the following example:

- *Right, footprint is the compound word. Paleontologists learn about dinosaurs by examining their footprints.*

Writing: This writing activity is linked to the footprint activity described in the science section below.

- Create a Dinosaur: After students have created their footprint, they can draw a picture of the dinosaur, which they can name using their own first name (Jasonsaurus). Have students label the drawing and then write a description of the dinosaur, including what it eats and how it protects itself. This will give your students the opportunities to use target words, such as *plates, shields, spikes, teeth,* and so on.

Math: As you have seen with other books in this section, it is usually fairly simple to construct word problems that use the target words.

- *A paleontologist found 6 bones from a tyrannosaurus rex, 3 bones from a triceratops, and 5 bones from an iguanodon. How many bones did she find in all?*

Remind your students that the tyrannosaurus had teeth that were 6 inches long. Prepare a simple worksheet with teeth of different lengths for students to measure and then identify the one that would have come from the T. rex.

Science: After reading and discussing the last page about dinosaur footprints and the information that scientists get from them, give each child a small lump of play clay. Students can press the clay into a plastic lid or in the bottom of a milk carton that has been trimmed down on the sides. They can then use their fingers or plastic spoons or knives to make an imprint that depicts a dinosaur footprint. Use this activity to discuss fossils, and then have your students complete the writing activity described above.

If possible, locate fossils for your science center for students to explore. You may find that your families are a great resource for this. Many museum stores have inexpensive packets with fossils for students to examine. Although it was not a fossil, my students enjoyed studying a shark jaw bone that my son had purchased as a souvenir on a family beach outing. I did not tell them what animal the bone belonged to; I let them act as paleontologists to see what they could learn about the animal from studying this "fossil."

Using Read-Alouds to Teach Vocabulary © 2011 by Karen J. Kindle, Scholastic Teaching Resources

A 5-W + H activity helps students learn more about one particular word by answering the questions *Who? What? When? Where? Why?* and *How?* I often use a simple graphic organizer in the shape of a hand; a W question goes in each finger, and the H question is in the palm. The following example shows possible questions and answers based on this text:

- Who? Paleontologist

- What? Search for and dig up fossils

- When? Still doing this—starting 200 years ago

- Where? Places where the dinosaurs lived (locate places)

- Why? So they can learn more about dinosaurs and maybe what happened to them

- How? Use brooms, pick axes, shovels, chisels to chip the bones out of the rocks

Cafeteria: As students are eating lunch, you might make comments on whether they are being carnivores or herbivores, using dinosaur names in the process.

- *You are eating chicken for lunch today. Is that a lunch that a **brontosaurus** or an **allosaurus** would like?*

- *Your salad looks so good! I'll bet an **apatosaurus** would like that since they were **herbivores** and only ate plants.*

UNIT 7

Chameleon, Chameleon *by Joy Cowley*

Text description: *Follow the chameleon on his search for food. Although this text reads like a narrative, it is an informational text that tells about the habitat of the chameleon, how it catches its food, and how it changes colors to communicate. The incredible photographs in this text are great for discussing facts about chameleons, colors, and textures. You will find the information at the end of the text most helpful in answering the questions that are sure to come from your students. The text is very simple, so your students will enjoy reading it independently. The narrative style will be familiar to young children. Eric Carle's* The Mixed-up Chameleon *would make a nice companion fiction story for this book.*

Vocabulary for Instruction

Possible target words: chameleon, rests, peaceful, juicy, insect, scary, gecko, creeps, danger, dangerous, either, branch, suddenly, scorpion, stinger, poisonous, carefully, caterpillar, zap, angry, chew, greets, welcomes, pale, tree frog

Animals: chameleon, insect, gecko, scorpion, caterpillar, tree frog

Words with morphemes: This set of words is very helpful if you are showing your students how we add suffixes to words to create new words: peaceful, scary, dangerous, stinger, poisonous, suddenly

Miscellaneous: rests, peaceful, juicy, scary, creeps, danger, dangerous, stinger, poisonous, gulp, branch, suddenly, zap, chew, greets, welcomes, pale

During Reading

The simplicity of *Chameleon, Chameleon* makes it ideal for reading to younger learners. Each time you read it, students will learn more and more about chameleons and notice other details in the photographs. Consider limiting your strategies to *labeling* the first time through, and then adding other strategies on subsequent readings. Be sure to match the words you draw attention to during your reading and the words you focus on for infusion activities that day; for example, if you focus on words with morphemes during your reading, include them in your infusion activities as well. A mixture of strategies is presented in the following suggestions:

- *The chameleon is **resting**. He is sleeping. See how his eyes are closed?* (synonym)

- *This kind of **chameleon** is a panther chameleon. The males are about fifteen inches long.* (extension)

- ***Chameleons** have very special eyes. They can look in different directions at the same time. Can we do that?* (extension)

- *He wants a nice, juicy **insect**. What are some things you like to eat that are **juicy**?* (examples)

- *Look carefully at the chameleon's feet. They help him hang onto the tree **branch** when he is climbing up and down.* (extension)

- *Does the **gecko** look **scary** to you? Can you make a scary face like the gecko? What is something that scares you?* (imagery, questioning, examples)

- *This **gecko** is a leaf gecko.* (labeling) *Do you think that is a good name for him? Look in this picture—can you see him? His tail looks just like a dried up leaf.* (questioning/extension)

Using Read-Alouds to Teach Vocabulary © 2011 by Karen J. Kindle, Scholastic Teaching Resources

- *This is the **scorpion**. (labeling) He has a **stinger** (labeling) on the end of his tail that is **poisonous**. That means it is full of poison. If the scorpion stung the **chameleon**, he would probably die. Can you think of any other animals that are poisonous? (examples)*

- *It says that the chameleon is creeping. It looks like it is tiptoeing in this picture. So I am thinking that to **creep** means to go very quietly and slowly. (context, definition) He is very **carefully** creeping past the **scorpion** so the scorpion won't notice him.*

- *His tongue works like a frog's, doesn't it? He **zaps** out his tongue and then pulls the **caterpillar** back in just as fast. (extension)*

- *Chameleons' colors change to communicate their moods. This **chameleon** isn't sure about the stranger, so her colors are dark and **angry**. (extension)*

- *Pale colors. Light colors. (synonym) **Pale** and dark are opposites. Can you think of some pale colors? Some dark colors? (examples)*

- *The way **chameleons** change colors is almost like talking—or the way we use our faces to show that we are **angry**, happy, or afraid. (extension) How would your face look if you were the chameleon and you were trying to tell a stranger to go away? How would you look if you were showing that you were friendly? (imagery)*

- *Do you remember how we said that a **chameleon's** eyes can look in different directions at the same time? You can see that really well in this picture. See how this eye is looking straight at us, but the other eye is still looking to the side to watch for danger? (extension)*

Infusion Activities

Categories: Brainstorm lists of words that fit the following categories: insects, things that are juicy, things that are colorful, things that are dangerous, and so on.

Odd Man Out:

- *brown, black, white, purple* (White is a pale color.)

- *angry, happy, upset, mad* (Happy is the opposite of the other moods.)

Analogies:

- Black is to dark as pink is to _____. (**pale**)

- Cracker is to dry as peach is to _____. (**juicy**)

Line It Up: There are a lot of words you can select for this game. One game possibility is shown below using the words *rest, juicy, creep, peaceful, branch,* and *harm.* Students move the cards down to the bottom of their desks, placing them in a line from left to right.

- *When you do this, you are quiet and still—you may even be sleeping, like the chameleon. This card is first.* (rest)

- *The second word describes something that has lots of moisture in it, such as a pear or a peach.* (juicy)

- *When you do this, you move very quietly and carefully so no one will notice you. This card goes in the third spot.* (creep)

- *The fourth word is the opposite of angry or upset.* (peaceful)

- *The fifth word is a part of a tree that the chameleon climbs on.* (branch)

- *Something that is dangerous may do this to you. It is a synonym for* hurt. *This is the final word.* (harm)

Clothesline: There are several possibilities for clothesline activities related to this unit.

- After students have brainstormed a list of color words, choose a group and have students order the words from pale to dark.

- Select words from the list of emotions you made in the Act It Out activity below and have students put them in order from happy to sad.

Act It Out: Extend the discussion of emotions the chameleons portrayed in the text. Begin the activity by brainstorming a list of emotions; then have students add additional examples. They can then select an emotion and act it out for their classmates to guess.

Phonological and phonemic awareness: There are several words in this text that are helpful to use in teaching morphemic analysis. Students are in the process of learning how we add suffixes to words to create new words and how those suffixes change the word's use. It may be a good time to infuse a discussion of the *-ous* suffix into your lessons, using the words *dangerous* and *poisonous* from the text. Write the two words on the board or on sentence strips and ask students to identify the part of the word that is the same. Explain that the *-ous* suffix means "having the quality of"—it turns a noun into an adjective, so something that is dangerous is full of danger and something that is poisonous is full of poison. Provide a few other examples such as *wondrous* and *marvelous.* You can extend the activity as shown below.

- Collect and use *-ous* words: *famous, humorous, wondrous*

- Repeat with *-ful* words: *peaceful, wonderful, flavorful, delightful*

Using Read-Alouds to Teach Vocabulary © 2011 by Karen J. Kindle, Scholastic Teaching Resources

Writing: Using effective adjectives in writing descriptions is a commonly taught skill in the primary grades. This activity can be done as an interactive writing for kindergarten and first-grade students, and as an independent writing activity for second graders.

- Describe the chameleon: *Let's look really carefully at the chameleon. What are all the colors we can see?*

- This is a great time to use that 64-pack of crayons to match the vivid colors of the chameleon. There are several shades of blue, green, orange, and yellow pictured.

- *Look at the texture of the chameleon's skin. Does it look as if it would feel rough or feel smooth to your touch? What do you think a chameleon's skin might feel like? Would it be rough like sandpaper or do you think it would feel like bubble wrap?*

- Draw or paint a chameleon, using pointillist techniques: Students finger paint with an index finger or an eraser tip, a marker just touching tip to the paper, or a crayon coloring little dots. If your students go to an art teacher for specials, you may want to enlist his or her help with this activity. Ask students to write a sentence or two telling about their chameleon's colors and what these colors mean about his mood. These sentences give the students an opportunity to use some of their new vocabulary; for example:

  - My chameleon has happy colors because he has a branch for his home.
  - My chameleon has scared colors because he sees a poisonous scorpion.

Science/Social Studies: The panther chameleon is native to Madagascar. Your students may be familiar with the animated movies of the same name. Show them where Madagascar is on a map or globe. What would the habitat be like there? Would it be hot or cold? Why?

UNIT 8

Into the A, B, Sea *by Deborah Lee Rose*

Text description: *Students in the primary grades enjoy alphabet books, and this one with its wonderful illustrations by Steve Jenkins and engaging text is sure to become a class favorite. In addition to being a source for ocean animals, the vivid verbs that Deborah Lee Rose uses present great opportunities for useful vocabulary words. Eric Carle's* A House for a Hermit Crab *makes a nice* *companion piece for this text. Once again, the information on each animal in the back of* Into the A, B, Sea *will be invaluable and is a source of some great vocabulary words as well!*

Vocabulary for Instruction

There are almost too many with this fun text, but here's a sampling!

Possible target words: *ocean, waves, dive, anemones, sting, barnacles, cling, crawl, dolphins, spin, eels, explore, soar, whale, peep, humpback, leap, insects, prance, jellies, kelp, forest, sway, leopard sharks, prey, manatees, lumber, narwhals, slumber, octopuses, penguins, glide, queen angels, glow, rays, swoop, grab, nab, umbrellamouths, dine, viperfish, shine, exhale, yellowfin, zillion, zooplankton, thrive, wonders*

Animals: *anemones, barnacles, dolphins, eels, flying fish, gray whales, humpbacks, jellies, leopard sharks, manatees, narwhals, octopuses, penguins, queen angels, rays, sea stars, tiger sharks, umbrellamouths, viperfish, blue whales, yellowfin, zooplankton*

Action words: *sting, cling, spin, soar, peep, leap, prance, sway, prey, lumber, slumber, glide, glow, swoop, grab, nab, shine, exhale, thrive*

Rhyming pairs: *sting/cling, in/spin, explore/soar, peep/leap, prance/dance, sway/ prey, lumber/slumber, hide/glide, glow/low, grab/nab, dine/shine, exhale/whale, dive/thrive*

During Reading

Since this is a text you will undoubtedly want to read over and over again with your students, you can really change up your strategies with each reading. For example, during one reading you might use imagery to focus on the action words and in another reading, you may focus on the information about the animals.

Labeling will probably not be needed for this text, since the simple illustrations show only one animal at a time. However, if you are providing additional information in an extension, you might use labeling at this point. For example, when talking about the whale, you might say something like this:

- *Do you see this hole on the top of the **whale's** head? This is called a blowhole, and it is how the **whale** breathes. The blowhole is kind of like the **whale's** nose.*

As you plan your extensions, the information located in the back of the book will be very

Using Read-Alouds to Teach Vocabulary © 2011 by Karen J. Kindle, Scholastic Teaching Resources

helpful. This section is another source of great vocabulary words. The following description shows an example:

- *"Spinner dolphins are the ocean's best gymnasts, twirling and somersaulting high over the waves before falling gracefully back into the sea."* (Words such as *twirling, somersaulting,* and *gracefully* would be great infusion words.)

Depending on your students' ages and interests, you might provide only one or two facts about each animal, or explore one or two animals in more depth. Some suggestions are given below to get you started.

- *Have you seen* **dolphins spin** *like that? What other tricks have you seen them do?* (questioning, examples)

- *The* **eel** *has a very different kind of fin. How does it move through the water?* (questioning/extension)

- *In some places in the ocean,* **kelp,** *which is a kind of sea plant, grows like a* **forest**—*tall and all together like trees in the woods. The kelp grows very fast— almost a foot each day!* (definition, extension)

- *Do the* **manatees** *remind you of any other sea animals? I think they look a little like seals or walruses, except that their faces look more like bull dogs. Seals move very quickly in the water, but manatees* **lumber,** *which means they move pretty slowly and not very gracefully.* (extension, definition)

- **Narwhals** *are a kind of whale. Can you tell why they are called the unicorns of the sea? Even though this looks like a horn, it is actually a tooth, like an elephant's tusk.* (questioning, extension)

- **Octopuses** *have two ways that they can hide from predators—animals that try to eat them. First, they can squirt out a blob of ink in the shape of an octopus, which confuses their enemies, and they can slip away. They can also change color, like a chameleon, for camouflage.* (extension)

- **Penguins** *can look kind of silly on land. They waddle and can't move very fast on their feet. But on their bellies, they slide quickly and* **glide** *right into the water, where they are graceful and speedy.* (extension)

- *Is* **tiger shark** *a good name for this shark? Why? The* **leopard shark** *has spots like a leopard, and the tiger shark has stripes like a tiger.* (extension)

- *These fish live in the deep, deep parts of the* **ocean** *where very little light can reach—see how dark it is in the picture?* (extension)

- *Why do you think this one is called an* **umbrellamouth**? (questioning/extension)

- *The* **viperfish** *has its own fishing pole built in. Here on the end of this long fin is a special tip that glows in the dark like a lure. When other fish try to catch it, the viperfish grabs them with its huge teeth.* (extension)

- *Just like us,* **whales** *breathe air, even though they live in the ocean. They inhale* (breathe in to demonstrate) *and* **exhale** (breathe out). *They have a blowhole on the top of their heads. When they come up for air, they first have to exhale and blow water out—that's what you see here in the picture that looks like smoke. The mothers have to help their babies at first so they will know how to breathe.* (imagery, extension)

- **Yellowfin** *is certainly a good name for this type of tuna. Have you ever eaten a tuna sandwich?* (questioning)

- *A tuna has lots of fins. The fins help the tuna swim and change directions in the water.* (extension)

- **Zooplankton** *are tiny, tiny sea animals—and what is really strange is that they are the favorite meal for whales!* (definition, extension)

- **Thrive** *means "to do really well." It means the animals are finding everything they need to grow and live and that there are lots and lots of them.* (definition)

- *A* **zillion** *is a really, really big number. We have millions, and billions, and trillions—zillions would even be more than those numbers!* (definition)

Infusion Activities

Categories: Prior to reading the book, ask students to brainstorm a list of all the animals they know that live in the sea. Keep the list and add to it after reading the text.

Analogies: Create simple analogies to help students see similarities and differences between different animals.

- **Octopus** is to 8 as **sea star** is to _____. (5)

- **Leopard shark** is to spots as **tiger shark** is to _____. (stripes)

Line It Up: Select six animals from the text and create word cards for them; for example, you might select *octopus, dolphin, penguin, eel, anemone,* and *whale.* Use the information in the back of the book to develop your clues as in the following examples:

- *The first word is the largest animal in the ocean.* (whale)

- *The second word is a fish that is long and thin like a snake.* (eel)

- *This animal looks like a flower or plant.* (anemone) *This is the third word.*

- *The fourth word is a sea animal that has eight legs.* (octopus)

- *This animal is a bird, but it can swim like a fish.* (penguin) *Put this word in the fifth spot.*

- *This mammal is very smart and can be trained to do lots of acrobatic tricks.* (dolphin) *This word goes in the last place.*

Using Read-Alouds to Teach Vocabulary © 2011 by Karen J. Kindle, Scholastic Teaching Resources

You can repeat this game on subsequent days with other animal names or with verbs; for example: *exhale, cling, spin, dine, slumber, sway.*

- *When you breathe in, you inhale. When you breathe out, you _____.* (exhale)
- *This word means to stick to or to hold on to something tightly.* (cling)
- *This word is a fancy way of saying* eat. (dine)
- *Another word for* sleep *is _____.* (slumber)
- *When you turn around and around very fast, you _____.* (spin)
- *This word means to move back and forth.* (sway)

Act It Out: Review the motions you used for the various action words in the text during your read-aloud. Students can then select words to act out for others to guess. To reinforce word recognition, you can also have students pick cards at random that have the words printed on them.

As a variation, you can give a child the name of an animal and have him or her perform the action associated with that animal in the text. For example, you might whisper the word *dolphin* to the child, and he or she would spin. Other students then guess which animal is being depicted.

Phonological and phonemic awareness: This text lends itself perfectly to bingo. Have the students make an eight square with a plain piece of paper and select eight different consonants, writing one in each square. Write each animal name from the text on a strip of paper. As you call the animal name on a given strip, add a sentence or two that provides information, for example:

- /y/ as in yellowfin: *A yellowfin is a type of tuna.*
- /v/ as in viperfish: *A viperfish has a special little light that lures fish close to its mouth.*

The rhymes included in this text make it perfect for practicing that phonemic awareness skill. During one reading of the text, focus on the rhyme pattern, omitting the final word of each couplet for the students to fill in.

- *"Swim the ocean waves with me and dive into the A, B, _____".* (sea)
- *"Where anemones sting and barnacles _____."* (cling)

Some of the spelling patterns included in this text are high-frequency phonograms that will be easy for your students to work with such as *ing, ine, ide, in, ow,* and *ale.* For more proficient spellers, you can create word sorts exploring the *ore* and *oar* patterns, *ee* and *ea,* or *ay* and *ey* using the target words from the text as your category headers.

Writing: Challenge your students to experiment with paper collage like the kind Steve Jenkins uses in the illustrations in this text. Guide students by asking them to think about how the leopard sharks and the tiger sharks resemble leopards and tigers. Ask them to think about what a lion shark or an elephant shark might look like. What would a pinkfin tuna look like? Encourage your students to use their imaginations to create sea creatures, give them descriptive names, and then write about them.

You can also use a familiar pattern from a book such as *Brown Bear, Brown Bear, What Do You See?* (Martin, 1983) to create individual or class books about the sea.

- <u>White barnacle, white barnacle</u>, what do you see?

- I see a <u>red crab</u> looking at me.

Music: Using the pattern shown below as a model, you can sing through the whole book.

A-Swimming We Will Go
(*sung to the tune of "A-Hunting We Will Go"*)

A-swimming we will go, a-swimming we will go
Where anemones sting and barnacles cling
A-swimming we will go.

Continue substituting phrases from the text; for example:

- *Where insects dance and jellies prance*

- *Where octopuses hide and penguins glide*

- *Where crabs crawl in and dolphins spin*

UNIT 9

Gobble It Up! A Fun Song About Eating! *by Jim Arnosky*

Text description: *This engaging song will help your students understand concepts such as habitat, the food chain, and the needs of living creatures. The repetitive text, rhythm, and rhyme are sure to make the song a favorite. Be sure to spend time talking about the illustrations. They add to the story with interesting details and tell a story of their own.*

Using Read-Alouds to Teach Vocabulary © 2011 by Karen J. Kindle, Scholastic Teaching Resources

Vocabulary for Instruction

There are a lot of potential vocabulary words that are not in the text but are present in the illustrations. Don't forget those when planning your instruction.

> **Possible target words:** *wild, raccoon, bat, crawdad, crawl, mouse, snake, gobble, crunch, shells, crocodile, fool, duckling, survive, alive, hunt, great white shark, pelican, cruise, shallows, circle, schools, chomp, giant, squid, panda bear, rare, bamboo, shoot*
>
> **Animals:** *raccoon, crawdad, crocodile, duckling, great white shark, whale, squid, panda, pelican, bat, mouse, snake, coral*
>
> **Miscellaneous:** *crawl, gobble, crunch, fool, survive, hunt, cruise, shallows, circle, schools, chomp, rare, bamboo, shoot*

During Reading

Since so much of the story is told through the illustrations, you will probably use *labeling* a lot in your initial readings. For animals that your students are not familiar with, you will want to provide more information; for example, if you live in a part of the country where students know a lot about crawdads, you won't need to talk about them much and might use questioning as your strategy. But if your students have never seen crawdads, you will need to provide some information through *definitions* and *extensions*. Here are some suggestions:

- ***Raccoons*** *are nocturnal—that means they sleep during the day and are active at night. Can you think of other animals that are nocturnal?* (extension, examples)

- *Do you see another nocturnal animal in this picture?* (reverse labeling, example)

- *Have you ever seen* ***crawdads***? *Sometimes they are called crayfish or mudbugs.* (synonyms) *They look like little lobsters or kind of like shrimp with claws—but they live in fresh water instead of in the ocean.* (extension)

- *See how the* ***crawdads*** *have these hard shells?* (labeling) *The* ***raccoon*** *has sharp teeth so he can bite through them. It makes a* ***crunching*** *sound when he eats.* (extension) *What is something you eat that makes a crunching sound?* (examples)

- *It says that the* ***crocodile*** *is trying to* ***fool*** *the* ***ducklings***. *That means he is trying to trick them so they will come close enough for him to grab.* (definition)

- *Oh good, it looks like the* ***ducklings***—*the baby ducks—all got away. I can see a feather on the* ***crocodile's*** *snout, but I still can count four ducklings.* (synonym)

- *Is the **shark** really mean? I know he looks scary, but he is just doing what all animals have to do—hunt for or find food to eat. We all have to eat to **survive**.* (synonym, extension)

- *When the author says "school" is he talking about the kind of **school** we go to? No, a group a fish is called a school.* (definition)

- *What is a **circle**? A circle is a shape, and when we go around something, we move in that shape. So when it says that the shark **circles** the fish, it means he swims around them.* (definition) *Tommy, can you stand up and circle around James, as if you were a shark circling its prey?* (imagery)

- *Some animals, like **pandas**, eat plants or animals that grow only in certain places. Panda bears eat only **bamboo**, and bamboo is **rare**—that means it is not very common. So pandas can only live in places where they can find bamboo if they are going to **survive**.* (definition, extension)

- *It's a good thing that **bamboo** grows really fast! This **panda** ate the bamboo right down to the ground. All that is left are these little **shoots**.* (labeling, extension)

Infusion Activities

Categories: Because the list of animals in this text is rather short compared to the other texts we have been discussing, you may want to pull in other animals for sorting.

- Brainstorm a list of other animals and what they eat.

- Use the habitats mentioned in the text (woods, ocean, lake) as sorting categories for the animals you listed in the first activity. Add other habitats you've studied, such as polar regions, rainforest, and deserts.

- Sort animals as carnivores, herbivores, and omnivores.

Analogies: This text focuses on what various animals eat, so you may want to base your analogies on those relationships.

- **Panda** is to **bamboo** as **raccoon** is to _____. (**crawdad**)
- **Shark** is to carnivore as **panda** is to _____. (herbivore)
- **Raccoon** is to forest as whale is to _____. (ocean)

Line It Up: Make word cards for five or six target words, such as *fool, circle, crunch, rare,* and *school.* Develop a series of clues that focus on word meaning.

- *The first word is a synonym for* trick. *The crocodile tried to trick the ducklings by pretending to be asleep.* (fool)

Using Read-Alouds to Teach Vocabulary © 2011 by Karen J. Kindle, Scholastic Teaching Resources

- *The second word is a shape and an action. You do this when you go around and around something.* (circle)
- *You might make this noise when you are eating carrot and celery sticks.* (crunch) *This is the third word.*
- *A synonym for this word would be* unusual *or* uncommon. (rare) *This is the fourth word.*
- *The last word is the word we use for a group of fishes.* (school)

Writing: Students can write about their favorite foods. Model the use of target words by saying something like the following:

- *The crawdads that the raccoon likes to eat remind me of shrimp. That is one of my favorite foods. I am going to write about how I like to gobble up shrimp.*

Math: Infuse the target words into your daily word problems. Try having your students write their own problems using the animals from the story.

- *A school of 10 fish was swimming in the ocean. A hungry shark ate 2 fish and a pelican ate 1 fish. How many fish got away?*
- *The raccoon gobbled up 3 crawdads on Monday and 5 crawdads on Tuesday. How many crawdads did he gobble up?*

Music: *Gobble It Up!* comes with a CD that puts the text to music. With the song format already provided, it is easy to add additional verses. Take the list of animals that your students brainstormed in the Categories activities, add the foods that they eat, and adapt the text to fit; for example:

- *If a penguin you could be, you'd swim around in the cold, cold sea.*
  You'd look and look and wish and wish, and find yourself some tasty fish.

You can create another song by using students' names in place of the animals' and talking about the foods they like to eat. While it might not directly reinforce the vocabulary you have selected, it will provide you with opportunities to review the concept that all living things need food. And your students will have fun as well.

> If a boy named Marcus you could be, in your lunch box you would see,
>
> A sandwich and chips and carrots and dip,
>
> You'd eat it all up if you could. Yes you would, yes you would,
>
> You'd gobble it up and it'd taste good!

Science: Many of the illustrations in this text have layers of information that students can discuss. The illustrations can help reinforce science and social studies concepts and give additional opportunities to use and develop vocabulary. Students also learn to use illustration in nonfiction texts as a source of information (Stead, 2006). For example, on the first page of this text, students can learn a great deal about raccoons from studying the illustrations.

- *Where do raccoons live?*
- *When do they hunt for food?*
- *How do they catch their prey?*
- *Do you notice another animal on the page that is looking for food to gobble up?* (In the background, you can see a snake and on the far left a silhouette of a mouse scampering away.)
- *Notice the raccoon's long claws and sharp teeth.*
- *Is the water deep or shallow?*
- *How do you think the raccoon can find the crawdads under the water?*

As your students become more skillful in noticing more details, you can simply ask them what they notice and resort to asking questions after their responses.

If you normally teach the elements of the food pyramid, or talk about healthy eating habits, you can tie these topics nicely into this text as well. Have students plan a healthy meal that they would gobble up so they could survive.

Cafeteria: Since this text focuses on the things animals eat to stay alive, it will be easy to talk about the foods students gobble up to stay healthy. You might be able to generate new verses for the song by observing the foods particular students really seem to enjoy.

Using Read-Alouds to Teach Vocabulary © 2011 by Karen J. Kindle, Scholastic Teaching Resources

CHAPTER 6

Fiction Read-Aloud Units

Primary teachers usually have a wide selection of fiction texts that they use for read-alouds. I had a group of favorites that related to certain themes or objectives, which I kept out of the regular classroom library, introducing them to students during those units of instruction. Using the same books for read-alouds year after year helps you improve and extend your vocabulary instruction. As you work with students, you improve your unit as you learn which strategies are most effective for particular words. You can extend your instruction as you think of new ways to infuse your target words. It is also important to continue to find new texts to use for your read-alouds.

The vocabulary unit plans in this chapter introduce you to some texts you might be familiar with and gives you some ideas to get started. They provide suggestions for words you can target for instruction, specific strategies to use, and a variety of activities you can incorporate into your daily instruction. You can use these fiction read-aloud units as presented or adapt them to fit the needs of your students and your own personality. For more information on the unit format, see pages 44–45 in Chapter 5.

Each unit begins with a brief description of the text. In the section titled "Vocabulary for Instruction," you will find a list of potential target words. Additional word lists suggest specific categories that you can focus on, such as "Action words," "Multiple meaning words," and "Miscellaneous." These lists may contain a combination of possible target words and new words. You will still need to examine the words and determine whether they fall into Group 1, Group 2, or Group 3 (see Chapter 4, pages 35–36 for an explanation of this process). In most cases, there are many more possible words than you would want to target for instruction.

The next section, "During Reading," contains suggestions for questions you might incorporate in your reading to promote critical thinking and use of target vocabulary. Although you are the best judge of which strategies to use for your purposes and to meet the needs of your students, some general suggestions are included to facilitate the selection process.

The final section in each unit, "Infusion Activities," provides you with a variety of possible activities for infusing vocabulary instruction from the read-aloud throughout your day. It is by no means an exhaustive list. You will undoubtedly find additional ways to incorporate your target words into your daily routines.

UNIT 1

***Inside Mouse, Outside Mouse** by Lindsay Barrett George*

Text description: *This delightful book by Lindsay Barrett George is great for developing students' understanding of position words and antonyms. The text on alternate pages is printed in contrasting colors to help learners keep the opposite patterns of the book in mind.*

Position words and prepositional phrases can be particularly difficult for ELLs. Consider how prepositions are used in these examples.

- We walk **on** the beach, but walk **in** the woods.

- We fill **out** forms and fill **in** blanks.

The large pictures provide support for acquisition of some common Tier 1 words that newcomers to the English language might be learning, including *wall, rug, ground, table, cat, hare, chair, dog, squirrel, pencils, flowers, book, bird, socks, rock, spider, ball, hole, bat,* and *window.*

The final spread shows the big picture, and it is great for recapping the mice's journey.

Vocabulary for Instruction

Even though this is a relatively simple text, there are a lot of words to choose from.

> **Possible target words:** *inside, outside, stump, wall, down, across, rug, ground, under, next to, bush, hare, chair, front, squirrel, can, in, out, behind, book, bird, between, socks, rocks, below, spider, over, ball, stone, through, hole, along, bat, hose, around, flowers, house*
>
> **Position words:** *inside, outside, down, across, under, next to, up, in front, into, out, behind, between, below, over, through, along, around*

> **Antonyms:** *inside/outside, up/down, in front/behind, below/over, in/out*
>
> **Rhyming words:** *wall/ball, clock/sock/rock, hare/chair, cat/bat*
>
> **Multiple-meaning words:** *bat, can* (a can to hold pencils and a watering can), *wall* (in the house and the stone wall)

During Reading

Labeling and *imagery* are the most obvious strategy choices for this text. During the first reading, you might want to focus on labeling to be sure that your students are familiar with that vocabulary. It will be hard for them to understand how the mouse goes along the hose if they cannot identify the hose. If you have a lot of ELL students, you will use basic labeling, but if you have students who have greater language proficiency, you might use some reverse labeling as well. During the second reading, you will want to focus more on the prepositions by using imagery. Use your hand to trace the mouse's actions as you read the words.

For your students who have greater language proficiency, here are some questions you might ask during reading that will challenge their thinking and also prompt the use of vocabulary as they express their thoughts.

- *Why are the numbers backwards on the* **clock**? (The mouse is inside the clock.) (questioning)

- *What things does the house mouse have* **inside** *his nest?* (Students might mention the Q-tip, pretzel, cookie, bits of string, M&Ms, kernels of rice, lint.) (questioning/labeling)

- *What is a stump? Look carefully at the illustration and think about the story.* (It is **outside**; it is made of wood; it has a hole to the outside.) (questioning)

- *What is another word for* **rug**? (carpet) (synonym)

- *What are some of the things you see in the picture as the* **outside** *mouse runs across the* **ground**? (questioning/labeling)

- *How are the nests of the two mice the same? How are they different?* (questioning)

- *The* **inside** *mouse ran up a* **wall**, *and the* **outside** *mouse ran up a wall. How are the walls different? What does the outside wall look like it is made of?* (questioning/extension)

- *Both mice run* **in** *and* **out** *of a* **can**. *How are the cans different? What do you use each one for?* (questioning/extension)

- *What is different on this page?* (The view looks **down** from above—aerial view) (questioning)

Infusion Activities

Categories: Have your students help you brainstorm lists of things that are outside and things that are inside. Start with the items in the illustrations and then add to them from students' knowledge and experiences. Use these words for a series of sorts such as the following:

- Sort living and nonliving things

- Sort inside and outside animals from the story (mouse, spider, ant, grasshopper, snail, cat, hare, dog, squirrel, bird, centipede, caterpillar, beetle, worm, toad)

- Sort inside and outside items from the story (clock, stump, socks, rocks, ball, stone, wall, rug, ground, table, bush, chair, can, book, hole, bat, hose, flowers)

Analogies: The words in this text are well suited to analogies dealing with synonyms and antonyms.

- **Inside** is to **outside** as **up** is to _____. (**down**)

- **Rock** is to **stone** as **hare** is to _____. (rabbit)

- **Under** is to **over** as **below** is to _____. (above)

Line It Up: Each child will need six index cards or strips of paper with the words *up, down, under, next to, between,* and *around* written on them. Use a rubber mouse or a picture of a mouse and demonstrate the actions indicated below. Use the following clues or make up your own version:

- *In the first place, put the card that shows where the mouse is going.* (up the wall)

- *Where is the mouse now? Put that card in the second position.* (place the mouse under a chair)

- *Which word describes where the mouse is now? Place that card in the third spot.* (place the mouse between two books)

- *What is he doing now? That card is in the fourth position.* (make the mouse go around and around your head)

- *The mouse is on my shoulder; now he is going . . .* (move the mouse down your arm) *Put that card in the last place.*

Using Read-Alouds to Teach Vocabulary © 2011 by Karen J. Kindle, Scholastic Teaching Resources

Repeat the game with different cards and/or different clues.

Act It Out: You can use the same rubber or paper mouse from the Line It Up activity and have students act out various position words for their classmates to guess.

Phonological and phonemic awareness: There are many activities you can infuse with target words from this text to provide additional practice.

- *Rhyming:* Write the words from one of the rhyme pairs on the board or a chart. Have students generate additional rhymes to fit the pattern. This can be done orally or in written form.

- *Isolation of initial and final phonemes:* Use target words for these activities to provide additional familiarity for students. Be sure to add some word meanings as you go through the exercises.

  - *What sound do you hear at the end of* clock, sock, *and* rock?
  - *Listen carefully to these words:* chair, hare, stone. *Which one doesn't rhyme?*

Writing: Students can use the pattern of the story to create their own books using the target propositions. You may also want to read *Rosie's Walk* (Hutchins, 1971), a similar text, for ideas.

- A Mouse in My House: Provide each student with a four- to eight-page blank booklet. These could be made in the shape of a house. Students can plan the mouse's journey through the house, drawing pictures to match. List the position words on a chart or word bank for support with spelling.

- Variation: A Mouse in My Yard: Students complete the book as described above with things they would have outside in their yards.

Music: This text is easy to put to music. Here are two possible songs for you to use. The first is an adaptation of the familiar tune, "Hickory, Dickory, Dock," and the second is sung to the tune of "Twinkle, Twinkle Little Star." Have your students help think of motions and/or additional verses.

Hickory, Dickory, Dock *(an adaptation)*

Hickory, dickory, dock,	Hickory, dickory, dug,	Hickory, dickory, dee,
the mouse slept in the clock.	The mouse ran across the rug.	The mouse ran behind the tree.
The clock struck one and down he ran	The clock struck two, he climbed into my shoe	The clock struck three and the mouse saw a bee
Hickory, dickory, dock.	Hickory, dickory, dug.	Hickory, dickory, dee.

Little Mouse

(sung to the tune of "Twinkle, Twinkle, Little Star")

Scurry, scamper, little mouse,

What are you doing in my house?

Under the table and up the wall,

Across the rug and down the hall,

Scurry, scamper, little mouse,

What are you doing in my house?

Scurry, scamper, little mouse,

What are you doing in my house?

Along the bat and between the socks,

In front of the dog and back to the clock,

Scurry, scamper, little mouse,

What are you doing in my house?

Recess: Create two simple mouse hats by attaching circles to sentence strips. Make one hat in gray for the inside mouse and one in brown for the outside mouse. Divide the class into two teams. Create a simple obstacle course using the position words from the text. List the steps on sentences strips and place them in a pocket chart. This way you can change the order and make a whole new game. The exact steps that you choose will depend on the configuration of your room. This can be adapted for outside play as well. Here are some sample directions.

- Run across the rug.
- Run between the desks.
- Run under the table.
- Run around the chairs.
- Run in front of the chalkboard.
- Run behind the easel.

Using Read-Alouds to Teach Vocabulary © 2011 by Karen J. Kindle, Scholastic Teaching Resources

UNIT 2

Skippyjon Jones by Judy Schachner

Text description: Skippyjon Jones *is one of a series of books by Judy Schachner about a Siamese kitten with a vivid imagination which takes him on all sorts of adventures. In this book, Skippyjon imagines that he is not a cat, but a Chihuahua—the famous sword fighter, El Skippito. He saves the Chimichangos from the desperado Alfredo Buzzito, a giant bumblebee who is stealing their beans.*

Although our youngest learners will not "get" all of the humor and word play in this wonderful series, there are plenty of opportunities to build vocabulary and help them understand as they are able. If you have students who are familiar with Spanish, they will particularly enjoy the plays on words.

Vocabulary for Instruction

Possible target words: *please, ordered, self-respecting, britches, flock, scolded, birdbath, lecture, bounce, Siamese, gigantic, shot, exclaimed, rifled, bandito, mellow, lonesome, desert, journey, Chihuahuas, incognito, whispered, secret, password, decreed, outraged, somber, landscape, scattered, shimmied, chattered, castanets, thrust, ruckus, thrust*

Multiple-meaning words: *please, order, rifle*

Spanish words: *buenas noches, mis amigos, hola, muchachitos, muy, guacamole, Chihuahua, bandito, caramba, poquito, sí, gracias, adíos, loco, frijoles, por qué, yo quiero, vamos, sombrero*

Animals: *bird, grouse, mouse, moose, goose, bat, rat*

Rhyming words: *mouse/grouse, moose/goose, rat/bat, fiesta/siesta*

Words to use in dialogue: *cried, whispered, declared, decreed, ordered, scolded, exclaimed, called*

During Reading

This text is a bit long, so you will want to keep your interruptions to a minimum, particularly during the first reading. Use labeling and imagery where possible since they do not interfere with your reading. Look for places to use your voice effectively to demonstrate word meaning as shown below:

- "Alfredo Buzzito," **whispered** the crowd.

- "Not your beans!" **cried** Skippito, outraged.

- Then in a **muy, muy, soft voice**, he said, "My name is Skippito Friskito."

Insert gestures and facial expressions where you can to demonstrate word meaning.

- . . . he **thrust** his sword into the air.

- Then they took a **siesta**.

- His legs **shimmied** and shook like the Jell-o and his teeth **chattered** like castanets.

Here are some additional questions and comments you might use during subsequent readings.

- *When the text says that Skippyjon climbed onto his mouse—what is it talking about?* (context)

- *What is a **fiesta**? What clues do you find in the picture?* (context)

- *What is a **siesta**? What clues are there in the picture?* (context)

- *Why do Skippyjon's legs **shimmy** and his teeth **chatter**?* (questioning)

Infusion Activities

Categories: Generate lists of words that can be used later for sorting activities. Here are some suggestions.

- Sort beans: red, black, baked, cocoa, coffee, kidney, pinto, jelly

- Sort breeds of cats

- Sort breeds of dogs

- Sort types of candy you would find in a piñata

- Sort things you would see at a fiesta

Analogies: Some analogies are based on object/classification relationships. The following examples help students think of a category in which to place each term.

- **Siamese** is to cat as **Chihuahua** is to _____. (dog)

- **Frijole** is to bean as **sombrero** is to _____. (hat)

Using Read-Alouds to Teach Vocabulary © 2011 by Karen J. Kindle, Scholastic Teaching Resources

Line It Up: Make word cards for the following words: *bounce, journey, flock, incognito, whisper, somber.*

- *The first word means a very long trip.* (journey)

- *The second word is what we call a group of birds.* (flock)

- *The third word is the opposite of* shout. (whisper)

- *The fourth word is a synonym for* serious. (somber)

- *The fifth word is something you can do with a ball.* (bounce)

- *The last word means you are wearing a disguise so that no one will know who you are.* (incognito)

Phonological and phonemic awareness: If your students have learned about suffixes, you can have fun with the word play in this text using the *-ito* suffix. As you read the story, have students listen for words that include the *-ito* suffix. They can engage in word play and add the suffix to English words just like Skippyjon does.

- *How would Skippito say paper?* (paperito)

Writing: Young writers need practice writing dialogue and using words other than *said* in their work. Encourage their creativity by having them write dialogue between Skippyjon and a character of their choice. You can make simple puppets and have students use them to create the dialogue first, then write it down. Brainstorm a list of possible words to use instead of *said*, starting with the ones used in the book.

Music: You can substitute words in Skippyjon's song. Also, make maracas and castanets and learn the Mexican Hat Dance with your students. You can make maracas from milk cartons that have been cleaned and dried. Put a handful of dried beans or rice inside and seal the carton well with tape. Students can then decorate the outside and shake their maracas to the music.

My name is Skippito Friskito. (clap clap) (alternating heels, arms folded)

I fear not a single bandito. (clap, clap)

My name is Skippito Friskito. (clap clap)

I fear not a single bandito. (clap, clap)

My manners are mellow, I'm sweet like the Jell-o, I get the job done yes indeed-o.

(link arms with partner, circle around)

My manners are mellow, I'm sweet like the Jell-O-o, I get the job done yes indeed-o.

Repeat first four lines.

Recess: Take the Mexican Hat Dance outside. Sing it faster and faster each time, and your students will really get the wigglitos out!

Cafeteria: Continue the word play into the cafeteria.

- *Be sure you drink all your milkito!*
- *You have a sandwichito and chipitos for lunch today.*

UNIT 3

Snowmen at Night by Carolyn Buehner

Text description: *I love this book! In the fanciful text, a little boy notices that the snowman he made the day before looks a little droopy, and he begins to wonder what snowmen do at night. The illustrations are filled with detail and humor; you will find new things each time you read the text. The illustrator has also hidden shapes in the snow (cat, rabbit, Santa face, T. rex) that your students will enjoy looking for, so be sure to spend a lot of time talking about the pictures.*

There are so many rich vocabulary words to add into your discussions that you will find one or two readings will not be enough.

Vocabulary for Instruction

Many of the words you can target for instruction will arise in the course of your discussions rather than just from the text. The suggestions below include "in the text" words as well as "outside the text" words.

> **Possible target words:** *wintry, looked a fright, wonder, slide, lawn, gather, sipping, anxious, pond, pitcher, aim, by far, thrill, tuckered out, crooked, height, cocoa, giggling, slipped, drooped*
>
> **Winter clothing:** *hat, scarf, muffler, boots, mittens, glove, earmuffs*
>
> **Rhyming words:** *fright/night/height/sight/fight, dark/park, others/mothers, places/races, twice/ice, clown/down, aim/game, hill/thrill, so/go*

Using Read-Alouds to Teach Vocabulary © 2011 by Karen J. Kindle, Scholastic Teaching Resources

During Reading

You will probably not use many extensions or clarifications with this book. If your students are already pretty familiar with snow and winter activities, you may want to pursue more questioning and context strategies as a means of assessing their prior knowledge. Always be sure when using questioning to have simple definitions ready in case your students start guessing. You do not want them to hear several wrong definitions before they hear the right one!

If your students do not have much experience with snow, or are ELLs with limited English proficiency, you will want to incorporate more labeling and imagery on the first reading and then mix in synonyms, definitions, and questioning on subsequent readings. As in many of the texts in this book, there are too many words to address in one sitting, so you will want to plan for multiple readings. That way, you can cover more words, focusing on a different set in each reading.

Here are some suggestions for your read-aloud comments.

- While reading the first page, use imagery to illustrate the meaning of *slipped* and *drooped*. Then follow with a comment such as the following: *His **hat** wasn't sitting on top of his head anymore—it had **slipped** to one side. And instead of sticking out straight, his arms had **drooped** down.* (imagery)

- *When it says he **looked a fright**, the boy means he didn't look right at all.* (definition) *Look here on the ground. He has dropped his broom and **mitten**.* (labeling) *This looks like one of his buttons or part of his mouth. His carrot nose is drooping, too. He looks a fright.*

- *So the boy started to **wonder**—he started to think.* (synonym)

- *Here is one snowman sliding off the **lawn**—that is the grass or yard outside your house.* (definition)

- *See how the snowmen are **gathering** in a circle here? Look how the mothers are pouring the **cocoa**—the chocolate milk—into cups.* (synonym)

- *This **pond** is all frozen. Now they are skating on the ice. But they don't even need skates. They can slip and slide without skates. Look at all the tricks they are doing!* (labeling)

- *They are sure having fun. How do I know that? See how they are laughing? It says they are **giggling**—that is another word for laughing.* (context/synonym)

- *Which snowman is the **pitcher**? When people play baseball, they use special gloves called mitts* (definition, labeling) *to protect their hands from the hard ball.* (extension) *What are the snowmen using for mitts?* (questioning)

- *What are the snowmen using to sled down the hill?* (questioning)

- *Oh my, look how tired the snowmen look. They are all* **tuckered out**. *You can see it is starting to get light, so it is almost morning. They have been playing hard all night, and they are getting sleepy.* (context)

Infusion Activities

Categories: You can think of many categories to use for brainstorming activities related to this text. Study the illustrations for categories, too. Once the lists have been constructed, you can sort them in various ways, including the following:

- Winter clothing
- Winter sports
- Things you need to make a snowman
- Things you can do in the snow

Analogies: The relationships in these analogies focus on function. Your students may need additional support if making snowmen and wearing winter clothes are unfamiliar to them.

- Carrot is to nose as sticks are to _____. (arms)
- **Hat** is to head as **mittens** are to _____. (hands)
- **Scarf** is to **muffler** as **hat** is to _____. (*earmuffs*)

Line It Up: For added fun, you might want to make the word cards for this unit from a die-cut snowman shape. Clues for two word sets are provided below. The first set focuses on winter clothing items (*scarf, hat, mitten, boots, earmuffs, gloves*) and the second one on more challenging words (*anxious, thrill, crooked, wonder, giggling, gather*). Students place each word in the order in which it is called.

Set 1

- *This is something you put around your neck to keep warm in the winter.* (scarf)
- *You put this on your head when it is cold.* (hat)
- *These keep your ears warm.* (earmuffs)
- *On a snowy day, you want to have these on your feet.* (boots)
- *You put this on your hand when it is cold. It has a special place for each finger.* (glove)
- *These go on your hands, too. They have a place for your thumb, but the other fingers are together.* (mittens)

 Using Read-Alouds to Teach Vocabulary © 2011 by Karen J. Kindle, Scholastic Teaching Resources

Set 2

- *Synonyms for this word are* nervous *or* excited. (anxious)
- *If you are doing this, you are laughing.* (giggling)
- *This word means "to excite."* (thrill)
- *The opposite of this word is* straight. (crooked)
- *This word means "to come together in a group."* (gather)
- *When you do this, you are asking yourself a question about something.* (wonder)

Act It Out: Students can take turns acting out the different activities depicted in the book. You can write on cards, or simply ask students to act out their favorite parts of the book. You can also link this to the writing activity below by asking students to act out what their own snowman might do at night such as the following:

- Ice skating
- Playing baseball
- Having a snowball fight
- Making snow angels
- Sledding

Phonological and phonemic awareness: Take advantage of the rhymes in this text for phonemic awareness activities such as those given below:

- As you read through the text, use a cloze technique, pausing for students to supply the missing rhyming word.
- Using the rhyme patterns from the text, generate additional rhymes that fit the pattern.
- More advanced students can work with alternate spelling for the same rhyme such as *-ight*, *-eight*, and *-ite*.

Writing: Combine art and writing in this simple project. Students can use the illustrations in *Snowmen at Night* as inspiration for creating their own snowmen using the medium of your choice. Discuss the different articles of clothing the snowmen are wearing, such as scarves, mittens, earmuffs, and hats. You could extend vocabulary further by talking about different kinds of hats, such as top hats, cowboy hats, baseball caps, bowlers, and stocking caps. Point out that the snowman wearing the cowboy hat has a bandanna and a sheriff's badge. Even though most of the snowmen have carrots as noses, show your students that one snowman seems to have a pickle or cucumber as a nose. These discussions will spark their creativity. Once the artwork is complete, students can write stories about what their snowman does at night.

Math: Use the ideas from the story to create word problems. Here are some examples:

- *The snowmen want to play baseball. They need 2 teams, and each team must have 9 players. How many snowmen do they need to play baseball?*

- *The children want to make 4 snowmen. They need to make 3 large snowballs for each snowman. How many snowballs do they need to make?*

Science: If you live in a place where it snows, have your students help you make a small snowman. Bring the small snowman inside in a pan and let your students observe what happens. Use a stopwatch and time how long it takes the snowman to melt.

Recess: Play some snowman games while you are outside. For instance, you can play kickball instead of baseball and have snowman races or play the following game:

Snowman relay: Divide the class into two or more teams. Each team is then divided into two with half the students standing at each end of the space. For each team, you will need the following snowman garb: hat, scarf, mittens, earmuffs. Place the pile of clothes at the end you designate as the starting line. The first child in each line suits up and at the whistle runs across the space to his teammates. He or she quickly takes off the snowman garb and the next player puts it on. Repeat until all students have had a turn.

Cafeteria: You can find ways to bring a little of the vocabulary into your lunchtime conversations.

- *You are drinking chocolate milk today. It is just like the ice-cold cocoa that the snowmen were drinking in our story.*

- *Do you think your celery would make a good nose for a snowman?*

- *You need to eat your ice cream quickly. It is starting to melt just like our snowman did.*

Using Read-Alouds to Teach Vocabulary © 2011 by Karen J. Kindle, Scholastic Teaching Resources

UNIT 4

Pumpkin, Pumpkin by Jeanne Titherington

Text description: *During the fall, most primary classes spend time talking about pumpkins and will enjoy reading about how they grow from seed to pumpkin. In* Pumpkin, Pumpkin, *a little boy named Jamie plants a pumpkin seed and then watches as his pumpkin grows from a seed to a sprout and finally to a great big pumpkin. He carves his pumpkin for Halloween, being sure to save some seeds to plant next year.*

The simple language and large print make *Pumpkin, Pumpkin* ideal for beginning readers. This book has been around a long time, but is still a classroom favorite. *It's Pumpkin Time!*, described in Chapter 5, is a great companion nonfiction text.

Vocabulary for Instruction

Unlike many of the books in this chapter, the choices for target words in this text are rather narrow, which makes it excellent for use with beginning readers and makes your instructional decisions easy.

> **Possible target words:** *plant (planted), pumpkin, grew, seed, sprout, flower, pick (picked), scooped, pulp, carved, face, window, saved, spring, wagon*
>
> **Animals:** There are some animals in the illustrations that you might want to discuss with your students; they help give a sense of the relative size of the pumpkin plant: *ladybug, gopher, butterfly, rabbit, frog, mouse, goose, squirrel, dog*

During Reading

Again, this text is very simple with few words, so it is a good choice for students with limited vocabulary. The illustrations are good for labeling. If your students are more proficient, use questions and extensions.

- *This is the **pumpkin seed**.* (labeling) *It isn't very big, is it?*

- *Look how the author used the **pumpkin plant** to make the letter J for Jamie's name. Very clever!* (extension)

- *The **sprout** (labeling) is very tiny here, isn't it? It is so small that the **ladybug** (labeling) is taking up the whole leaf. The sprout is just the baby plant. It is going to grow and get much bigger.* (definition)

- *Look how the **sprout** has grown into the **plant**. Now it has lots of leaves, and this **gopher** can hide under the leaves.* (labeling)

- *This is the pumpkin **flower**.* (labeling) *It is orange like the **pumpkin** will be and is about the size of the butterfly. The flower shows where the pumpkin will grow.* (extension)

- *See here how the **flower** has dried up, and the little **pumpkin** is starting to grow. It is about the size of Jamie's ball.* (labeling, extension)

- *The **pumpkin** is even bigger than the basket now. Do you think these are Jamie's feet?* (questioning)

- *Look how big the **pumpkin** has become. It **grew** and grew—kept getting bigger and bigger—just like you are growing and getting bigger.* (extension)

- *Jamie's **pumpkin** is so big that he can't carry it. So he put it in his **wagon**.* (labeling)

- *Have you ever seen the inside of a **pumpkin**? Let's look inside this one I brought. We can see the **pulp** and the **seeds**.* (extension)

- *See how the pumpkin has a face now? Jamie's mom and dad helped him carve a face. They used a knife and cut these holes in the pumpkin for its eyes, nose, and mouth. They **carved** a **face**.* (labeling as you point to the facial features, definition)

- *Jamie **saved** some **seeds** for spring. That means he kept them to **plant** next year.* (definition)

Infusion Activities

Categories: You can build vocabulary with this story by generating lists of words in the categories shown below with students. After you have created the lists, you can take cards from each category and mix them up to use for sorts.

- Parts of a plant

- Plants that we eat (can further break into fruits and vegetables)

- Things we use in the garden

Analogies: The content of this text makes time-order relationships a natural focus.

- **Sprout** is to **plant** as child is to _____. (adult)

- Watermelon is to summer as **pumpkin** is to _____. (fall)

Using Read-Alouds to Teach Vocabulary © 2011 by Karen J. Kindle, Scholastic Teaching Resources

Line It Up: Use the words *plants, seed, sprout, flower, pumpkin,* and *carve* for this activity. Students will place the words in a line at the bottom of their desk in the order in which they are called.

- *It is small, and you put it in the ground to make your garden.* (seed)
- *This is a word for a baby plant.* (sprout)
- *This word describes lots of things that grow in your garden.* (plants)
- *This is a very pretty part of the plant. It shows where the pumpkin will grow.* (flower)
- *This is something you might do to your pumpkin to make a face on it.* (carve)
- *This fruit is big and orange.* (pumpkin)

Clothesline: Use the Clothesline activity to practice sequencing the events in this story. Write the words *seed, sprout, plant, flower,* and *pumpkin* on cards and then have students pin the cards in the correct order on the clothesline. You can repeat the activity with words associated with the actions in the story such as *plant, water, pick, carve, save.*

Picture It: Students who are having difficulty identifying the vocabulary words will benefit from drawing pictures on the word cards. After students have made their individual set of cards, help them draw pictures of the seed, sprout, plant, flower, and pumpkin. Bring in some pumpkin seeds for students to glue on the card for *seed.*

Phonological and phonemic awareness: The target words for this text have some useful spelling patterns for beginning readers. Students can use these patterns to generate more words in a variety of spelling activities.

- Brainstorm lists of words that rhyme with *seed, sprout,* and *plant.*
- Use letter tiles or magnetic letters to practice phoneme substitution.
  - Start with the word *seed.*
  - Change a letter to make *need.*
  - Change a letter to make *deed.*
  - Change a letter to make *feed.*
  - Change a letter to make *feet.*

Writing: There are many published thematic units available that will give you ideas for writing activities associated with pumpkins. You may want to consider linking writing and science by having your students plant seeds and record their observations in a science journal.

The following activity is one that my classes have always enjoyed. Create individual booklets for each child. I use die-cut pumpkin shapes to make it a bit easier. Students can use the following pattern for the text of their books. On each page, they add the facial features mentioned.

- *I carved my pumpkin for Halloween.*
- *My pumpkin has two _____eyes.* (Add a describing word on each page.)
- *My pumpkin has one _____nose.*
- *My pumpkin has a _____ mouth.*
- *My pumpkin looks _____.*

Math: Use pumpkin seeds as manipulatives for addition and subtraction problems. Students can write equations and then glue the correct number of seeds on the page to illustrate. You can also use pumpkins and seeds in your word problems.

- *Jamie planted 2 rows of pumpkin seeds. He planted 4 seeds in each row. How many pumpkin seeds did he plant?*

Music: The vocabulary in this book is similar to that in *It's Pumpkin Time!*, which appears in Chapter 5. You can use the song for that unit, "It's Almost Pumpkin Time," with this text as well (see page 69).

Science: The vocabulary from this book can easily be incorporated into a unit of study on plants, which is common in curricula for young students.

- Build a Plant: This activity is a variation of Build a Cowboy (Kindle, 2008). Create simple cutout drawings that depict the parts of the pumpkin plant: roots, vine, leaf, bud, flower, sprout, pumpkin, and so on. This can be done on a flannel board or with magnetic strips, Velcro dots, or ticky tack. As you talk about each part and its function, place it on the board, building up the completed plant. Include labels for the parts so that students will also see the words. By the end of the week, your students will be able to label a diagram of a plant and write or talk about the parts and their functions.

- Have a variety of seeds for students to study with magnifying glasses. They can record their observations in a science journal.

- Create a matching game. Gather ten seeds of different shapes and sizes such as apple, avocado, lemon, and pumpkin. Have drawings or pictures of the full-grown plant on index cards. Students can then match the seeds to the correct fruit or plant.

Using Read-Alouds to Teach Vocabulary © 2011 by Karen J. Kindle, Scholastic Teaching Resources

UNIT 5

Saturday Night at the Dinosaur Stomp
by Carol Diggory Shields

Text description: *The rollicking rhythm and rhyme of this fun book make it a great read-aloud. All sorts of dinosaurs gather for a blow-out dance. This would be a great companion text for Gail Gibbons's* Dinosaurs, *described on pages 70–75 in Chapter 5. There are lots of places for students to become involved in the reading by joining in, for example: "Then iguanodon shouted, 'One, two, three!'"*

Students will enjoy the humor, such as the ankylosaurus using his club-like tail to drum on his back, the protoceratop's eggs walking along, or the old dinosaurs who have lost their teeth.

Vocabulary for Instruction

Possible target words: Dinosaur names appear below. *prehistoric, slick, slime, scales, romp, stomp, lava, tar pit, shore, trampled, tromped, tracks, paddled, bash, plodded, batch, bouncing, gossiping, bunch, punch, giggled, shuffled, stared, party, drummed, chorus, perform, blasted, tune, wink, spike, Triassic, Jurassic, conga line, capered, volcanoes, fireworks, earthquake, twirled, Cretaceous, Cenozoic, outrageous, dawned, beat, yawned, snoring, swamp*

Dinosaur names: *plesiosaurus, pterodactyl, protoceratops, diplodocus, maiasaur, iguanadon, brachiosaurus, supersaurus, ultrasaurus, ankylosaurus, pentaceratops, duckbill, allosaurus, tarchia, stegosaurus, brontosaurus, raptor, tyrannosaurus rex, carnosaurus*

Rhyming words: *slime/time, romp/stomp, shore/floor, nails/tails, tromp/stomp, splash/bash, eggs/legs, bunch/punch, stared/scared, three/tree, back/whack, rhyme/time, chance/dance, like/spike, bump/jump, glow/show, shake/quake, beat/feet*

Action words: *romp, stomp, scrub, brush, curl, trample, tromp, paddle, flew, plod, follow, count, gather, sit, sip, giggle, shuffle, stare, shout, sang, drum, blasted, stood, wink, dance, caper, twirl, yawn, snore*

During Reading

In order to preserve the rhythm and rhyme of this text as much as possible, you will want to limit your interactions during some readings to labeling and imagery. Use movement to illustrate the meanings of words such as *shuffle, winked,* and *twirled.* During subsequent readings, you will want to take more time for extensions, context, questioning, and other strategies.

Cloze techniques will be effective for helping students predict the rhymes. You can cover some of the rhymes with sticky notes and then peel them back for students to use letter/sound correspondences to confirm their predictions.

Be sure to have your students join in where appropriate; for example, they can use their knees as drums and join in with ankylosaurus in beating the rhythm to "Boomalacka, boomalacka! Whack! Whack! Whack!"

Some specific suggestions for your readings appear below. You would not want to use all of these ideas in the same reading; include a few different strategies with each reading.

- *These little dinosaurs are letting everyone know about the Dinosaur **Stomp**—a big dinosaur dance.* (synonyms)

- *They scrubbed their necks and **nails** (imagery), brushed their teeth and **curled** their **tails** (imagery). Does your mom ever curl her hair? The dinosaurs don't have hair, so they are going to curl their tails to look pretty for the party.*

- *These dinosaurs are in a hurry. Are they tiptoeing? No, they are **trampling** and **tromping** with their big, heavy feet. Let's tromp like a dinosaur would.* (imagery)

- *They are making **tracks**—footprints—in the dirt.* (synonym)

- ***Plesiosaurus paddled** up.* (imagery)

- *A **bash** is another word for a big party.* (synonym)

- ***Diplodocus** is a really big dinosaur with short legs. So when he walks, he doesn't move very fast, and his steps are heavy. He **plods**.* (definition)

- *She has a whole lot of babies, doesn't she? A big batch. Your mom might make a **batch** of cookies. She doesn't just bake one or two cookies, she bakes a whole batch.* (synonym)

- *Look carefully at these dinosaurs. What do you notice about them? You're right! They don't have any teeth. They are the old dinosaurs.* (questioning)

- *What does it sound like when you **giggle**?* (imagery)

- *Show me what you look like when you **stare** at someone.* (imagery)

- *We learned that this dinosaur has bony plates on his back like a shell. He is using them for a drum.* (extension)

Using Read-Alouds to Teach Vocabulary © 2011 by Karen J. Kindle, Scholastic Teaching Resources

- *Triceratops has three horns. How many horns does* **pentaceratops** *have?* Penta- *means "five." A pentagon has five sides—a pentaceratops has five horns.* (extension)

- *See how they are all in a line with their hands on each other's shoulders? That is a* **conga line**. (labeling, definition)

- *The* **volcanoes** (labeling) *are erupting and throwing lava up into the sky like the* **fireworks** *that you might see on the Fourth of July.*

- *The dinosaurs were tired and* **beat**. Beat *can mean "to hit a drum," but here it means that they were all worn out.* (definition)

Infusion Activities

Categories: These suggestions are only a few ideas for the activities you can develop for brainstorming, sorting, and categorization.

- Brainstorming
  - Things you do to get ready for a party
  - Dinosaur names
- Sorts
  - Take the action words and sort them into categories such as ways of moving or things you do when you are tired.
  - Carnivores and herbivores
- Odd Man Out
  - *stomp, trample, plod, dance* (*Dance* means "a graceful movement.")
  - *scrub, brush, wink, curl* (Wink is not something you do to get ready for a party.)

Analogies: There are many possibilities for analogies in the target words. Select the ones that are most appropriate for your students.

- **Giggle** is to nervous as **yawn** is to _____. (sleepy)
- **Beat** is to **drum** as strum is to _____. (guitar)
- **Triceratops** is to triangle as **pentaceratops** is to _____. (pentagon)

Line It Up: The only hard part of making a Line It Up activity for this book is narrowing your choices down to only five or six words. Here is one suggestion for the words *wink, yawn, snore, batch,* and *shuffle.* As always in this activity, students place their word cards in the order in which you give the clues.

- *This word is something you do with one eye.* (wink)

- *You might do this while you are sleeping.* (snore)

- *This is something you do when you are tired.* (yawn)

- *This word means "a big group."* (batch)

- *When I move like this, without lifting my feet off the ground, I do this.* (shuffle)

Clothesline: Take some of the action words from the story that describe movement. Start with *plod, fly,* and *shuffle.* Have students help you put these words on the clothesline in order from slow to fast. Ask them to help generate other ways of moving to fill in the gaps.

Act It Out: This text has lots of great action words that are perfect for acting out. You can either write words on cards for students to select, or you can have them choose from a list or the pocket chart. They might act out the words *yawn, snore,* or *paddle* for their classmates to guess. Start with a short list of ten words and then add more words as your students learn them.

Phonological and phonemic awareness: Texts with strong rhyme patterns such as this one work well for phonemic awareness development. Many of the activities described in other sections of this book can be adapted for use with the vocabulary words in *Saturday Night at the Dinosaur Stomp.* Here are a few additional ideas.

- *I want to write in my journal that I brush my teeth every day, just like the dinosaurs. Let's stretch the word out and listen to the sounds: b-r-u-sh. The first sound is /b/. What letter makes that sound?* (continue with other sounds) *Let's look in the book and see if we can find the word* brush *and check if we are right.*

- Create a Making Words activity with *stegosaurus* as your mystery word. Use the following clues or make up your own:

  - *Make the word* rug.

  - *Change a letter to make* tug.

  - *Change a letter to make* tag.

  - *Change a letter to make* rag.

  - *Change a letter to make* sag.

  - *Change a letter to make* sat.

Continue with set, get, gets.

  - Put all of the letters together to make the name of a dinosaur.

 Using Read-Alouds to Teach Vocabulary © 2011 by Karen J. Kindle, Scholastic Teaching Resources

Math: Students know that a triangle has three sides, but they often don't realize that the prefix *tri-* means "three." Explain to your students that just as a tricycle has three wheels and a triangle has three sides, a triceratops has three horns. Draw a pentagon on the board and count its sides.

- *A pentagon has 5 sides. How many horns do you think a pentaceratops would have?*

Reinforce the learning with word problems such as the following:

- *A protoceratops has 1 horn, a triceratops has 3 horns, and a pentaceratops has 5 horns. How many horns is that altogether?*

Music and Recess: Create a dinosaur dance of your own that students can use to get the wiggles out. Find some music with a good, strong beat and work in some dance steps from the book. Start with the Triassic Twist and then do the Brontosaurus Bump, the Raptor Rap, and the Jurassic Jump. You can have the steps planned in advance, or ask students to come up with ideas.

Science: Although this book is big on fun, it is a bit short on facts. If you are using this text in conjunction with a nonfiction book, you may want to consider using some of the activities described in the unit in Chapter 5 for *Dinosaurs* by Gail Gibbons.

UNIT 6

The Three Little Wolves and the Big Bad Pig *by Eugene Trivizas*

Text description: *In this version of the well-known fairy tale, pig and wolf reverse roles. Three cuddly, little wolves build a series of increasingly strong houses to stay away from the big bad pig. In the end, the wolves find that the weakest house of all causes a change of heart in the pig, and they all live happily ever after.*

Students enjoy hearing stories that are based on familiar tales. Their existing schema for this story helps them understand the humor and appreciate the irony at the end. If your students are not familiar with the story of the three little pigs, you will want to read that first.

Vocabulary for Instruction

As with many longer stories, particularly narratives, this text is full of rich vocabulary. You will have many options for target words. You may want to consider revisiting this text for another round of read-alouds later in the year and focus on a whole different set of words.

Possible target words: *cuddly, fluffy, beware, wheelbarrow, certainly, prowling, croquet, grunted, china, fetched, sledgehammer, escape, beaver, crumbled, concrete, concrete mixer, slurry, battledore, shuttlecock, pneumatic drill, smashed, trembling, determined, barbed wire, iron bars, armor plates, padlocks, Plexiglas, chains, generous, kindhearted, extremely, securest, absolutely, hopscotch, bolted, dynamite, fuse, scorched, marigolds, daffodils, roses, cherry blossoms, ceiling, sunflowers, daisies, water lilies, buttercups, fragile, swayed, bluebell, scent, fantastic, fragrant, tender, tarantella, piggy-in-the-middle, strawberries, wolfberries, accepted*

Animals: *wolf, wolves, pig, kangaroo, beaver, rhinoceros, flamingo*

Actions: *prowl, grunt, fetch, escape, crumble, smash, tremble, bolt, scorch, sway, accept*

Adjectives: *cuddly, fluffy, generous, kindhearted, secure, fragile, fantastic, fragrant, tender*

Compound words: *wheelbarrow, sledgehammer, battledore, shuttlecock, padlock, kindhearted, hopscotch, sunflowers, buttercups, bluebell, strawberry, wolfberry*

During Reading

This story is quite long, so you may want to consider breaking it up into chunks and reading only one portion per day. The logical stopping places would be after each house has been destroyed by the big bad pig. This is a great text for using different voices as you read, and its familiar pattern encourages students to join in to huff and puff along with the pig.

Because of the length of the story, you will probably want to do most of your vocabulary instruction before or after reading, when you can more thoroughly build the concepts. Many of the words are abstract and will be difficult for students with limited language, so you will need to take more time and present lots of examples. For instance, you may want to help your students understand the concept of generosity.

- *The rhinoceros was very* **generous**. *He gave the little wolves lots of things to help build their houses. He was happy to share with them. Yesterday, when Monica didn't have a pencil, Sarah gave her one. That was very generous of Sarah. Can you think of a time when you were generous to someone?* (examples)

Here are some other ideas to include in your read-aloud of this text.

- *These little* **wolves** *are soft and* **cuddly**, *just like a puppy would be. You just want to hold them close and cuddle because they feel so soft and fluffy.* (extension, imagery)

 Using Read-Alouds to Teach Vocabulary © 2011 by Karen J. Kindle, Scholastic Teaching Resources

- *Mother **wolf** tells them to **beware** of the big bad pig. What do you think beware means? Right, she is saying to be careful.* (questioning, definition)

- *This isn't like the story we know, is it? They are starting off building a strong house of bricks.* (labeling) *See the bricks here in the **wheelbarrow**?* (labeling)

- *Oh, my—look at the pig's face. He doesn't look very nice. It says he is **prowling**. That means he is sneaking around looking for something.* (definition)

- *This is a word that is new. It says that the little wolves were playing **croquet** in the garden. This picture shows the wolves outside, and it looks like they are playing a game. It looks like they are using these mallets to hit the balls through these wickets. I'll bet this is croquet.* (context)

- *The pig grunted. Can you **grunt** like a pig?* (imagery)

- *Look at his **sledgehammer**— a really big hammer for knocking things down.* (labeling)

- *Look here—the **wolves** are sneaking out with their teapot.* (labeling) *They are **escaping**—getting away from the pig.* (synonym)

- *Now, a brick house is pretty strong. What could they make their house from that would be stronger than brick?* (questioning/examples)

- *What are they using?* (questioning) *Is **concrete** strong? What are some things that are made from concrete?* (examples)

- *Hmmm. **Battledore** and **shuttlecock**. Think about the story and see what you think those words might mean. Look at the illustrations and listen as I read this part again: "They were playing battledore and shuttlecock in the garden."* (context)

- *Sometimes you see workmen using these drills to chop up the cement on a road. See how he is shaking? They are very strong and VERY loud.* (labeling, extension)

- *Look how the **wolves** are **escaping** this time. They tied the sheets together like a rope. And of course, they have their teapot!* (extension/context)

- *Can you think of something stronger than **concrete**? They are going to build their house of steel. Look—they have **chains**, and **barbed wire**, and all these locks for the door.* (labeling)

- *This house is very **secure**—very safe.* (synonym)

- *Their poor little tails are **scorched**. See how the tips are burned from the explosion? They did save their teapot though!* (synonyms)

- *Not even this house could keep out the big bad pig. What can they try next?* (questioning)

- *So now they are going to use flowers to make their house. Is that a good idea?* (questioning)

- *Are flowers strong? No, they are **fragile**—very delicate. It doesn't take much to break or damage a flower, does it?* (synonym, extension)

- *What would happen to a flower house in the wind? Right, it would **sway** back and forth. Sway back and forth in your places with me.* (imagery)

- *How do you think this house would smell? The pig thought it was **fantastic**! Not just good, but really, really wonderful!* (synonym)

Infusion Activities

Categories: There are many possibilities for categories with this text. You might want to create lists that can be posted around the room for some categories, such as the compound words. Students can add to these lists as they encounter compound words in other texts.

- Begin with the flowers used to build the three little wolves' house. Brainstorm additional flower names.

- Brainstorm a list of compound words starting with the text words.

- List things that are strong, starting with concrete, iron, and other items from the book.

Odd Man Out:

- *daffodil, rose, marigold, concrete* (Concrete is not a flower.)

- *iron, chain, cotton, concrete* (Cotton is not hard or strong.)

- *tender, generous, kindhearted, mean* (Mean is not a positive characteristic.)

Analogies: The examples provided here include a variety of relationships, and thus would be best for students who have had prior experience with analogies.

- Flower is to **fragile** as iron is to _____. (strong)

- **Croquet** is to game as tarantella is to _____. (dance)

- **Fantastic** is to good as terrible is to _____. (bad)

- Flamingo is to bird as **marigold** is to _____. (flower)

Line It Up: Make word cards for the following words: *generous, sway, crumble, certainly, fragile.*

- *The first word is the opposite of* greedy. (generous)

- *In the second place, put the word that is something a cookie might do.* (crumble)

Using Read-Alouds to Teach Vocabulary © 2011 by Karen J. Kindle, Scholastic Teaching Resources

- *The third word is a synonym for* surely. (certainly)
- *The fourth word is something trees might do in the wind.* (sway)
- *In the last place, put the word that is a synonym for* delicate. (fragile)

Clothesline: Help your students think about shades of meaning by putting the following words in order on the clothesline: *fantastic, horrible, good, bad, wonderful, great, awful.*

Act It Out: There are many words in this book that are appropriate for acting out. Students can act out *hopscotch, shuttlecock, croquet, huff and puff, trembling,* and *dancing a tarantella.* They might depict the pig *prowling,* or *sniffing,* or the house made of flowers *swaying* in the wind.

Picture It: Some of the target words are perfect for making picture cards. Students can write the word *fluffy* and glue cotton balls on the letters. The word *scorched* can be written to look as though the letters have been burned. *Puff* can be written in bubble letters, and *trembling* can be written with a shaky hand.

Phonological and phonemic awareness: It is not difficult to find words from this story that are appropriate for work on various phonemic and phonological awareness tasks. Here are two suggestions.

- Develop student's deletion abilities using words from the story. Start with compound words and then increase the difficulty by focusing on specific phonemes.
    - *Say* bluebell. *Say it without* blue.
    - *Say* teapot. *Say it without* tea.
    - *Say* sway. *Say it without* /s/.
    - *Say* chin. *Say it without* /ch/.

- Prepare a list of flower names representing all of the letters of the alphabet, and play a bingo game for initial phonemes.
    - *Cover the letter you hear at the beginning of* zinnia: /z/.
    - *Daffodils are yellow flowers that bloom in the spring:* /d/ daffodil.

Writing: Review the compound words from the text such as *buttercup, sunflower, bluebell,* and *strawberry.* Add additional words such as *blackberry* and *blueberry.* Students can make compound word pop-up books. On the front, the child would write *sun + flower =* (illustrating each part). On the inside, the child would draw a sunflower and glue it to the pop-up flap and write the new word, *sunflower,* underneath. Encourage students to be creative and make up their own flowers or berries.

- *What might a moonflower look like?*
- *What might a starflower or a redbell look like?*

Music: At the end of the story, the pig has a change of heart and becomes so happy he begins to dance the *tarantella*. Ask your music teacher or search the Internet for examples of tarantellas to play for your class. Students might enjoy listening to the music while completing some of their writing or drawing. They might be interested to know that people used to believe that doing this dance would cure the bite of a tarantula, which is how it got its name.

Recess: Teach your class to play some of the games that the little wolves played in the story. Many of your students will already know how to play hopscotch. You can teach them Piggy-in-the-Middle (change the name to Keep Away if you want). If your P.E. teacher has badminton rackets, or if you have them at home, you can make a game where everyone has a chance to hit the birdie. See if you can borrow a croquet set from a parent and demonstrate that as well (with careful supervision, of course). You may want to set up various stations so groups of students are smaller and more manageable.

UNIT 7

Mañana, Iguana by Ann Whitford Paul

Text description: *Your students will quickly recognize that this story is a version of the Little Red Hen. Iguana decides to have a party and invite all her friends. She enlists the aid of Conejo (Rabbit), Tortuga (Turtle), and Culebra (Snake) to send out invitations, decorate for the party, and prepare the food. She gets angrier and angrier as her friends give excuse after excuse for not helping. When it is time for the party, Iguana will not let her friends join in the fun, and they must watch from a distance. After the party, the three friends feel bad and do all the work to clean up the mess while Iguana sleeps.*

This is a great text to use if you have ELLs who speak Spanish as their home language. They will shine as they get to become the teachers. Spanish words are sprinkled into the text in a supportive manner that fosters the development of using context to determine word meaning; for example: *"Conejo hopped up and down."* Since the sentence states that *Conejo* is hopping, and the illustration shows a rabbit, it is easy for the students to determine that *conejo* means "rabbit" in Spanish. Examples like this are present throughout the text.

A glossary with a pronunciation guide is included at the beginning of the book to help you with pronunciation of the Spanish words.

Vocabulary for Instruction

> **Possible target words:** *twitched, celebrate, spring, party, rattle, shook, must, invitations, wriggled, deliver, pass, fidgeted, stuff, excuses, flounced, slapped, sighed, begged, streamers, smacked, puffed, decorate, guests, whipped, angry, cactus, shrunk, slithered, yawned, stretched, silent, scrubbed, platter, squiggled, squirmed, twitch, leftovers*
>
> **Spanish words:** *lunes, martes, miércoles, jueves, viernes, sábado, domingo, mañana, fiesta, piñata, iguana, conejo, tortuga, culebra, yo no, gracias, sí*

During Reading

This is a great text for teaching students how to use context clues to determine the meaning of unfamiliar words. As you saw in the example on page 116, the author is very careful to use recasting, predictability, illustrations, and context in a way that doesn't seem contrived or artificial.

In recasts, the English word or phrase is provided immediately before or after the Spanish as you can see in the following examples:

- *"On Monday, lunes, Iguana twitched her tail happily."*
- *"'Yo no. Not I,' said Conejo."*

In other cases, the English words are separated from the Spanish with a bit of dialogue, but the context is clear enough to help students see the connection. For instance, on the first page of text, Iguana suggests to her friends that they "celebrate spring with a party on Saturday." After Conejo agrees, Tortuga says, "A fiesta? On sábado?" You can help your students use context to determine that a *fiesta* must be a party and *sábado* must be Saturday.

The use of the days of the week is an example of how predictability supports word learning. The story starts on *lunes*, Monday, and each day after that Iguana asks for help in another party-related task. Students can think back and use their knowledge of the days of the week to determine that *martes* is Tuesday and *jueves* is Thursday.

In reading this text, I would suggest focusing on context during one reading with other strategies worked in only as needed. Use different voices for your characters, and encourage students to join in with repetitive phrases such as *yo no* and *mañana, Iguana*.

On subsequent readings, you might focus on Iguana and how she expresses her frustration with her tail. She wriggles, fidgets, flounces, slaps, smacks, and whips her tail as her irritation with her friends increases. Use physical imagery to demonstrate the differences in these motions.

Some specific suggestions for instruction during your read-aloud appear below:

- *I know this is **Iguana**, but I am not sure who **Conejo**, **Tortuga**, and **Culebra** are. Let's see if we can use the illustrations and the words in the story to figure it out. I can see a rabbit, a turtle, and a snake, so I know that these must be Conejo, Tortuga, and Culebra. It says here that Conejo hopped up and down. So which one do you think would be Conejo? Tortuga pokes out of a shell, so he must be the turtle. It says that Culebra shakes his rattle, so he must be the snake. I can see a rattle on the tip of his tail right here.* (context)

- *Iguana wants her friends to help **deliver** the **invitations**. She has all these invitations, and she has to get them to her friends. Do you think they have a mail carrier in the desert? No, so she needs to deliver them, to take them, to her friends.* (synonym)

- *Now **Iguana** wants help to stuff the **piñata**. Look at the illustration. What is she holding? That must be the piñata. And since she wants to **stuff** it, you must put things inside. What do you think they will put inside?* (labeling/context/questioning)

- *Iguana has a box in her hands—the **streamers** must be inside. I am still not sure what they are, though. It says that she is going to hang them. Maybe we will get some clues later in the story.* (questioning, context)

- *Okay, look here. In the box, we can see these rolls of **streamers**, and in this picture, Iguana has hung them from the **cactuses**. So these must be the streamers.* (context) *Look, the **piñata** is hanging up too.* (extension)

Infusion Activities

Categories: Create lists of things you would need for a party, games you might play, and food that you might eat. Make a list of things to celebrate, such as birthdays and holidays.

- Sort English and Spanish words from the text.

- Sort items by holiday, such as things related to Thanksgiving, Halloween, or Christmas.

Odd Man Out:

- *Monday, September, Tuesday, Saturday* (September is a month.)

- *invitations, balloons, streamers, cactus* (Cactus is not something you have at a party.)

Using Read-Alouds to Teach Vocabulary © 2011 by Karen J. Kindle, Scholastic Teaching Resources

Analogies: Create analogies using the animals from the story. Incorporate Spanish words where possible to provide your students with additional practice.

- **Conejo** is to rabbit as **culebra** is to _____. (snake)
- **Piñata** is to **fiesta** as cake is to _____. (birthday party)
- Rabbit is to fast as turtle is to _____. (slow)
- Turtle is to shell as snake is to _____. (scales)

Line It Up: Create word cards for the following words: *guests, platter, leftovers, invitations, deliver,* and *celebrate.*

- *If you want to do this, you might have a party or fiesta. Put this card in the first spot.* (celebrate)
- *You need to make these so your friends will know about your party. This card goes in the second position.* (invitations)
- *Once you put your invitations in the mail, the mail carrier will do this. Put this word in the third place.* (deliver)
- *The friends who come to your party are called this. This word goes in the fourth spot.* (guests)
- *This is a big tray that you will put food on for your party. This is the fifth word in line.* (platter)
- *When the party is over, you might have some extra food. Put this word in the last place.* (leftovers)

Clothesline: In the text, Iguana expresses her mounting irritation with her friends through the movements of her tail. After children have read the story with you a few times, create a clothesline activity using the words *wriggles, fidgets, flounces, slaps, smacks,* and *whips.*

Act It Out: Instead of acting out certain words as you would in charades, this story lends itself perfectly to a dramatic retelling, puppets, or a readers' theater script. Students can take the roles of Iguana, Conejo, Tortuga, and Culebra.

Phonological and phonemic awareness: Beginning readers often have difficulty with the three different sounds for the suffix *-ed.* Use words from the text to help students learn about these differences. Prepare word cards with a variety of -ed words from the text. You might want to have students help you collect them during one reading.

- *Look at these* -ed *words as I say them:* twitched, begged, fidgeted. *How is the sound of* -ed *different in each of these words?*

- *Let's make three columns. We will look at some more of the –ed words from the story and decide if the -ed sounds like it does in* twitched, begged, *or* fidgeted. *This word is* asked. Asked: *Where shall we put this one?*

Writing: The events of this story include many familiar things, such as celebrating birthdays and having parties. Additionally, many children are familiar with other versions of the Little Red Hen. This familiarity gives them experiences to draw on in their writing.

- Review the story and discuss the things that Iguana did to celebrate spring. Brainstorm a list of holidays and special days that students celebrate. What types of things do they use to decorate? What special foods do they cook? Students can then write about their special day.

- In the story, Iguana makes invitations for her party. Talk about the kind of information that needs to be on an invitation. You may want to bring samples of invitations to show. Students can create their own invitations for a special day at school to send home to their families.

- If your students are more proficient, they will enjoy writing their own versions of the Little Red Hen story. Show them that the desert setting is the author's inspiration for the characters and the use of Spanish. What would the story be like if it took place at the South Pole or in the rainforest?

Math: Use the fiesta theme to write some word problems such as the following:

- *Iguana wants to invite 20 guests to her party. If the invitations come in packs of 8, how many packs will she need to buy? How many invitations will she have left over?*

- *Iguana is stuffing the piñata. She wants each guest to get 3 treats. If she has 5 guests, how many treats will she need to stuff inside the piñata?*

For another day, you might purchase a large bag of mixed candies or small toys that could be used to fill piñatas. Have students sort the items and create a graph to show how many items of each type are in the bag.

Science: This version of the Little Red Hen takes place in the desert. Learn more about the desert and the animals and plants that live there. Students can use nonfiction books on the desert to try to identify the guests at Iguana's fiesta.

Using Read-Alouds to Teach Vocabulary © 2011 by Karen J. Kindle, Scholastic Teaching Resources

UNIT 8

Fancy Nancy by Jane O'Connor

Text description: *Fancy Nancy loves all things fancy— the glitzier the better! There are several Fancy Nancy books in print; in this text, Nancy is a bit frustrated with her plain family and sets about to teach them how to be fancy.*

This is a great text for raising students' awareness of words—or word consciousness— and is sure to get them collecting fancy words from their reading and environment, and using fancy words in their writing and conversation.

Vocabulary for Instruction

There are a lot of fancy words to choose from in this text. Be sure to study the illustrations for more possibilities. Don't overlook some of the more basic "plain" words if you have students with more limited language proficiency.

> **Possible target words:** *fancy, fuchsia, plume, sprinkles, lace, lace-trimmed, frilly, toothpicks, princess, tiara, chandelier, stupendous, ad, fridge, accessories, posh, twirls, suggests, escort, limousine, chauffeur, arrive, pinkies, parfaits, sundaes, curtsy, sublime, merci, waiter, dressing gown, bathrobe*
>
> **Fancy words:** *fuchsia, plume, tiara, stupendous, accessories, posh, chauffeur, parfaits, dressing gown, sublime*

During Reading

During your first reading, you might want to just let the text speak for itself. The author has the "plain" synonyms built right in, so many words will need little instruction, as you can see in these two examples from early in the book.

- *"My favorite color is fuchsia. That's a fancy way of saying purple."*
- *"I like to write my name with a pen that has a plume. That's a fancy way of saying feather."*

In other readings you might want to repeat the plain and fancy word pairs after reading the page, and ask your students which one is plain and which is fancy.

- *Fuchsia and purple. Which one would Nancy like?*
- *Would Nancy rather write with a pen with a plume or with a feather?*

Consider bringing in examples of some of the items for students to see if you are not sure they will understand. The illustrations in the book have lots of detail, but it is often difficult to get a clear picture of what the word means if the concept is unfamiliar. For example, you might bring in a bit of lace, a frilly toothpick, some sprinkles, or a patent leather shoe.

Here are more suggestions for your read-aloud comments:

- *Do you like **sprinkles** on your ice cream? Sprinkles are the little colored bits of candy that people sometimes put on top of cookies or ice cream.* (definition) *Here are some sprinkles I had in my kitchen that I use when I make cookies. You just take a little bit and sprinkle them over the cookie or ice cream. Do you think that is why they are called sprinkles?* (extension)

- ***Lace** is a fancy trimming that you often see on girl's clothing.* (definition) *I see that Tonya has lace on her socks just like Fancy Nancy. I have lace on my shirt here—and this is a cloth napkin we use for fancy dinners at my house. It has lace, too. What are some other things that might have lace? Yes, sometimes curtains have lace.* (examples)

- *Nancy likes **frilly toothpicks**. I brought in two kinds of toothpicks to show you. This one is just a plain, wooden toothpick. But look at this fancy one. It has these little frills on the top to make it fancy.* (labeling)

Even though there are plenty of fancy words in the text, you might want to draw students' attention to some things that are included in the illustrations but that are not specifically mentioned.

- *Look how Nancy has made her room all **fancy**. She had just a plain bed, and now she has a **canopy** bed. This material above her head is called a canopy.* (labeling, definition)

- *Nancy is wearing a fancy scarf in this picture. It is all made of feathers and it is called a **boa**—a really fancy scarf!* (definition)

- *Nancy says that a princess is supposed to keep her **tiara** on. Look at the picture. What is tiara a fancy word for? Right, a tiara is a kind of a crown.* (questioning)

Using Read-Alouds to Teach Vocabulary © 2011 by Karen J. Kindle, Scholastic Teaching Resources

- *Nancy gave her doll a fancy name. She named her Chandelier. Did you know that a **chandelier** is a fancy kind of light?* (definition) *Have you see the lights that hang from the ceiling, maybe over the table?* (example) *Some of them have lots of sparkly glass. So a chandelier is a fancy light.*

Infusion Activities

Categories: Brainstorm lists of plain things and fancy things. The lists can then be mixed up and re-sorted. You might start with more specific categories such as plain and fancy clothes, plain and fancy food, and plain and fancy colors. If your students have sufficient background knowledge—either from personal experience or from media—you could list things you would see in a fancy restaurant and in a plain one to compare. Here are a few suggestions for sorting activities.

- Sort fancy words by nouns, verbs, and adjectives.
- Sort words by plain and fancy.

Analogies: Synonyms are used a great deal in this text, so they are an obvious choice for analogies.

- **Fuchsia** is to purple as **plume** is to _____. (feather)
- Driver is to **chauffeur** as car is to _____. (**limousine**)

Line It Up: Use the following "fancy" words to create a Line It Up game: *stupendous, limousine, sprinkles, parfait, accessories, fuchsia.*

- *This first word is a fancy ice cream sundae.* (parfait)
- *The second word is a fancy car.* (limousine)
- *The third word is a fancy way of saying* great. (stupendous)
- *If you want to have fancy cookies, you might put these on top. This is the fourth word.* (sprinkles)
- *The next word is a fancy way of saying* purple. (fuchsia)
- *If you want to dress fancy, you need lots of these. Put this word in the last place.* (accessories)

Clothesline: Brainstorm a list of fancy ways of saying good, such as *stupendous, great, marvelous, wonderful,* and *fantastic.* Do the same with words for *bad* and *okay.* Then select a few words from each set for a clothesline activity: *great, marvelous, mediocre, average, unpleasant, horrible.* Your students will have a wide range of "fancy" ways of saying *good* and *bad!*

Picture It: Make "fancy" word cards by adding accessories, such as glitter, sequins, and feathers. You can glue them on the outline of the letters, or just decorate the corners. Students will easily remember that *plume* is a fancy way of saying *feather* if a little feather is attached to the card.

Writing: Some books inspire writing activities, and *Fancy Nancy* is one of them.

- *The crayon box:* The giant packs of crayons are filled with "fancy" ways of saying variations of the eight basic colors. Reread the page where Fancy Nancy talks about her favorite color, fuchsia, as a fancy way of saying *purple*. Encourage students to use the "fancy" color names as they write about their favorite colors, foods, clothing—just about anything will do. Do not limit them to the colors in the box—they may surprise you with other colors they know and all their "fancy" speech.

- *Create Plain and Fancy flip books:* A flip book is made by folding a piece of paper in half lengthwise and then cutting slits in the top sheet to the fold to create flaps that can be lifted up. You can do three or four sections depending on the size of your paper. Three sections seems to work best for 8½" x 11" paper, but the longer sheets of manila paper or newsprint can handle four sections. On the top, students write a "plain" word and illustrate it. Then they lift up the flap and write the word the "fancy" way; for example, a child might write "blue" on the top and "cobalt" under the flap, or "car" and "limousine." You may want to brainstorm a list of possibilities or help your students use a thesaurus for ideas.

Math: Nancy's favorite color is fuchsia. Create a graph of your student's favorite colors— using "fancy" names, of course.

Music: Find two pieces of music to play for your students. One piece should be "plain," perhaps a simple folk tune with a guitar accompaniment. For your "fancy" piece, select an orchestral piece or something from an opera. Have students listen carefully and then talk about how the pieces are different.

Cafeteria: Continue the discussion on colors in the cafeteria and point out that the chocolate ice cream or pudding students are eating gives them a "fancy" way of saying *brown*, or that celery can give them a "fancy" way of saying *green*.

 Using Read-Alouds to Teach Vocabulary © 2011 by Karen J. Kindle, Scholastic Teaching Resources

References

Au, K . H. (1998). Constructivist approaches, phonics, and the literacy learning of students of diverse backgrounds. In T. Shanahan & F. Rodriguez-Brown (Eds.), *National Reading Conference Yearbook, 47*, pp. 1–21.

Avalos, M. A. (2006). No two learners are alike: Learners with linguistic and cultural differences. In J. S. Schumm (Ed.), *Reading assessment and instruction for all learners* (pp. 50–86). New York: Guilford.

Baumann, J. F., Kame'enui, E. J., & Ash, G. E. (2003). Research on vocabulary instruction: Votaire redux. In J. Flood, D. Lapp, J. R. Squire, & M. Jensen (Eds.), *Handbook on research on teaching the English language arts* (2nd ed., pp. 752–785). Mahwah, NJ: Erlbaum.

Biemiller, A. (2001). Teaching vocabulary: Early, direct, and sequential. *American Educator, 25*(1), 24–28.

Biemiller, A., & Boote, C. (2006). An effective method for building meaning vocabulary in primary grades. *Journal of Educational Psychology*, 98, 44–62.

Blachowicz, C. L., & Fisher, P. (2000). Vocabulary instruction. In M. Kamil, P. Mosenthal, P. D. Pearson, & R. Barr (Eds.), *Handbook of reading research: Volume III* (pp. 503–523). Mahwah, NJ: Erlbaum.

Carey, S. (1978). The child as word learner. In M. Halle, J. Bresnan, & G. A. Miller (Eds.), *Linguistic theory and psychological reality* (pp. 359–373). Cambridge, MA: MIT Press.

Carlisle, J. F. (2000). Awareness of the structure and meaning of morphologically complex words: Impact on reading. *Reading and Writing: An Interdisciplinary Journal, 12*, 169–190.

Cash, M. M., & Schumm, J. S. (2006). Making sense of knowledge: Comprehending expository text. In J. S. Schumm (Ed.), *Reading assessment and instruction for all learners* (pp. 262–296). New York: Guilford.

Chall, J. S., & Snow, C. E. (1988). Influences of reading in low-income students. *The Education Digest, 54*(1), 53–56.

Chiappone, L. L. (2006). The wonder of words: Learning and expanding vocabulary. In J. S. Schumm (Ed.), *Reading assessment and instruction for all learners*, (pp. 297–332). New York: Guilford.

Cummins, J. (1983). Language proficiency, biliteracy, and French immersion. *Canadian Journal of Education, 8*(2), 117–138.

Cunningham, P. (2000). *Phonics they use.* New York: Longman.

Dale, E. (1965). Vocabulary measurement: Techniques and main findings. *Elementary English, 42*, 895–901.

Duke, N. K. (2000). 3.6 minutes per day: The scarcity of informational texts in first grade. *Reading Research Quarterly, 35*, 202–224.

Durso, F. T., & Coggins, K. A. (1991). Organized instruction for the improvement of word knowledge skills. *Journal of Educational Psychology, 83*, 108–112.

Fisher, D., Flood, J., Lapp, D., & Frey, N. (2004). Interactive read-alouds: Is there a common set of implementation practices? *The Reading Teacher, 58*, 8–17.

Fountas, I. C., & Pinnell, G. S. (1996). *Guided reading: Good first teaching for all children.* Portsmouth, NH: Heinemann.

Fountas, I. C., & Pinnell, G. S. (2001). *Guiding readers and writers: Teaching comprehension, genre, and content literacy.* Portsmouth, NH: Heinemann.

Genesee, F. (1985). Second language learning through immersion: A review of U.S. programs. *Review of Educational Research, 55*(4), 541–561.

Graves, M. F. (1986). Vocabulary learning and instruction. In E. Z. Rothkopf & L. C. Ehri (Eds.), *Review of research in education* (Vol. 13, pp. 48–89). Washington, DC: American Educational Research Association.

Graves, M. F. (2006). *The vocabulary book: Learning and instruction.* New York: Teachers College Press.

Harmon, J. M., Wood, K. D., & Hedrick, W. B. (2006). *Instructional strategies for teaching content vocabulary.* Newark, DE: International Reading Association.

Hart, B., & Risely, R. T. (1995). *Meaningful differences in the everyday experiences of young American children.* Baltimore, MA: Brookes.

Hayes, D. P., & Ahrens, M. (1988). Vocabulary simplification for children: A special case of "motherese." *Journal of Child Language, 15*, 392–410.

Hickman, P., & Pollard-Durodola, S. D. (2009). *Dynamic read-aloud strategies for English learners: Building language and literacy in the primary grades.* Newark, DE: International Reading Association.

Hiebert, E. H. (1988). The role of literacy experiences in early childhood programs. *The Elementary School Journal, 89*(2), 161–171.

Hirsch, E. D. (2005). Reading comprehension requires knowledge—of words and the world. In Z. Fang (Ed.), *Literacy teaching and learning: Current issues and trends* (pp. 121–132). Upper Saddle River, NJ: Pearson.

Huff-Benkoski, K. A., & Greenwood, S. C. (1995). The use of word analogy with developing reading. *The Reading Teacher, 48*, 446–47.

International Reading Association & the National Association for the Education of Young Children (1998). Learning to read and write: Developmentally appropriate practices for young children. Retrieved electronically on September 3, 2008 from http://www.reading.org.

Juel, C., Biancarosa, G., Coker, D., & Deffes, R. (2003). Walking with Rosie: A cautionary tale of early reading instruction. *Educational Leadership, 60*(7), 12–18.

Kindle, K. J. (2008). *Teaching vocabulary in the K–2 classroom: Easy strategies for infusing vocabulary learning into morning meetings, transitions, centers, and more.* New York: Scholastic.

Using Read-Alouds to Teach Vocabulary © 2011 by Karen J. Kindle, Scholastic Teaching Resources

Krashen, S. (1985). *The input hypothesis: Implications and issues.* London: Longman.

Mason, J. M., Stahl, S. A., Au, K. H., & Herman, P. A. (2003). Reading: Children's developing knowledge of words. In J. Flood, D. Lapp, J. R. Squire, & J. M. Jensen (Eds.), *Handbook of research on teaching the English language arts* (2nd ed., pp. 914930). Mahwah, NJ: Erlbaum.

Morrow, L. M., Freitag, E., & Gambrell, L. B. (2009). *Using children's literature in preschool to develop comprehension.* Newark, DE: International Reading Association.

Nagy, W. E., & Scott, J. A. (2000). Vocabulary processes. In M. Kamil, P. Mosenthal, P. D. Pearson, & R. Barr (Eds.), *Handbook of reading research: Volume III* (pp. 269–284), Mahwah, NJ: Erlbaum.

Nation, K., & Snowling, M. J. (2004). Beyond phonological skills: Broader language skills contribute to the development of reading. *Journal of Research in Reading, 72*(4), 342–356.

National Center for Education Statistics (2000). *The condition of education.* Washington, DC: U.S. Department of Education.

National Reading Panel (2000). *Teaching children to read: An evidence-based assessment of the scientific research literature on reading and its implications for reading instruction.* Washington, DC: National Institute of Child Health and Human Development.

Neuman, S. B., & Dwyer, J. (2009). Missing in action: Vocabulary instruction in pre-K. *The Reading Teacher, 62*(5), 384–392.

Neuman, S. B., & Roskos, K. (1997). Literacy knowledge in practice: Contexts of participation for young writers and readers. *Reading Research Quarterly, 32*(1), 10–32.

Rog, L. J. (2007). *Marvelous minilessons for teaching beginning writing, K–3.* Newark, DE: International Reading Association.

Smith, B. D. (2007). *The reader's handbook: Reading strategies for college and everyday life.* New York: Pearson Longman.

Stanovich, K. E. (1986). Matthew effects in reading: Some consequences of individual differences in the acquisition of literacy. *Reading Research Quarterly, 21*, 360–406.

Stead, T. (2006, November). Keynote address. Texas State Reading Association, 35th Annual State Literacy conference, Austin, Texas.

Tompkins, G. E. (2006). *Literacy for the 21st century: Teaching reading and writing in prekindergarten through grade 4.* Upper Saddle River, NJ: Pearson.

Vanneman, A., Hamilton, L., Anderson, J. B., & Rahman, T. (2009). *Achievement gaps: How black and white students in public schools perform in mathematics and reading on the National Assessment of Educational Progress.* Retrieved July 22, 2009 from http://nces.ed.gov/nationsreportcard/pubs/studies/2009455.asp.

Vygotsky, L. S. (1962). *Thought and language.* Cambridge, MA: MIT Press.

Children's Literature Cited

Arnosky, J. (2008). *Gobble it up! A fun song about eating!* New York: Scholastic.

Buehner, C. (2002). *Snowmen at night.* New York: Scholastic.

Carle, E. (1991). *A house for hermit crab.* New York: Simon & Schuster.

Carle, E. (1984). *The mixed-up chameleon.* New York: HarperCollins.

Cowley, J. (2005). *Chameleon, chameleon.* New York: Scholastic.

Drew, D. (1997). *Tadpole diary.* Crystal Lake, IL: Rigby.

Fleming, D. (1993). *In the small, small, pond.* New York: Scholastic.

Gibbons, G. (1987). *Dinosaurs.* New York: Scholastic.

George, L. B. (2004). *Inside mouse, outside mouse.* New York: Scholastic.

Hall, Z. (1994). *It's pumpkin time!* New York: Scholastic.

Hutchins, P. (1971). *Rosie's walk.* New York: Aladdin.

Hutchins, P. (1993). *The wind blew.* New York: Aladdin.

Jenkins, S. (1995). *Biggest, strongest, fastest.* New York: Scholastic.

Jenkins, S. (1998). *Hottest, coldest, highest, deepest.* New York: Scholastic.

Jenkins, S., & Page, R. (2003). *What do you do with a tail like this?* New York: Scholastic.

Leedy, L. (2000). *Mapping Penny's world.* New York: Scholastic.

Marshall, J. (1990). *Hansel and Gretel.* New York: Scholastic.

Martin, B., Jr. (1983). *Brown bear, brown bear, what do you see?* New York: Henry Holt and Company.

Mayo, M., & Ayliffe, A. (2001). *Dig Dig digging.* New York: Scholastic.

Muth, Jon J. (2003). *Stone soup.* New York, Scholastic.

O'Connor, J. (2006). *Fancy Nancy.* New York: HarperCollins.

Paul, A. W. (2004). *Mañana, iguana.* New York: Scholastic.

Rose, D. L. (2000). *Into the A, B, sea.* New York: Scholastic.

Schachner, J. (2003). *Skippyjon Jones.* New York: Scholastic.

Shields, C. D. (1997). *Saturday night at the dinosaur stomp.* New York: Scholastic.

Titherington, J. (1986). *Pumpkin, pumpkin.* New York: Scholastic.

Trivizas, E. (1993). *The three little wolves and the big bad pig.* New York: Scholastic.

Van Laan, N. (2000). *When winter comes.* New York: Scholastic.

Yolen, J. (1998). *Welcome to the ice house.* New York: Scholastic.